WELCOME TO
NORMANDY & D-DAY BEACHES

Northern France is primed with possibilities – whether that means sampling Norman cheeses, getting close to WWI and WWII history or simply moseying around Rouen's old town. And with its abundance of coast and countryside, it's a pleasure to drive, too.

This is a region with a long (and turbulent) history that is plain to see. The scars of war can still be traced on the fields of Flanders and the beaches of Normandy. Elsewhere, be awed by the landscapes and villages that inspired artists such as Claude Monet.

Honfleur (p75)
YANN GUICHAOUA-PHOTOS/GETTY IMAGES ©

NORMANDY & D-DAY BEACHES

2 **Monet's Normandy**
Explore the landscapes and cities that inspired Monet. **4 DAYS**

1 **D-Day's Beaches**
Remember one of the biggest days in military history. **3 DAYS**

Eastbourne

Cap de la Hague

Cherbourg

Cotentin Peninsula

English Channel (La Manche)

Étretat

Côte d'Albâtre

SEINE-MARITIME

A29

Utah

D-Day Landing Beaches

Baie des Veys

Omaha   Gold

Baie de la Seine

Juno Sword

Côte Fleurie

Rade de Caen

Le Havre

Honfleur

Le Marais Vernier

Forêt de Cerisy

Bayeux

Caen

Ouistreham

Pont l'Évêque

Passage de la Déroute

St-Lô

Lisieux

Bernay

Coutances

MANCHE

CALVADOS

N158

Suisse Normande

Îles Chausey

Granville

Vire

Collines de Normandie

Falaise

Camembert

ORNE

Baie du Mont St-Michel

Flers

Parc Naturel Régional Normandie-Maine

Collines du Perche

Cancale

Mont St-Michel

Avranches

Forêt de Bellême

Alençon

BRITTANY

Rennes

Vitré

MAYENNE

SARTHE

A1

ILLE-ET-VILAINE

Laval

Le Mans

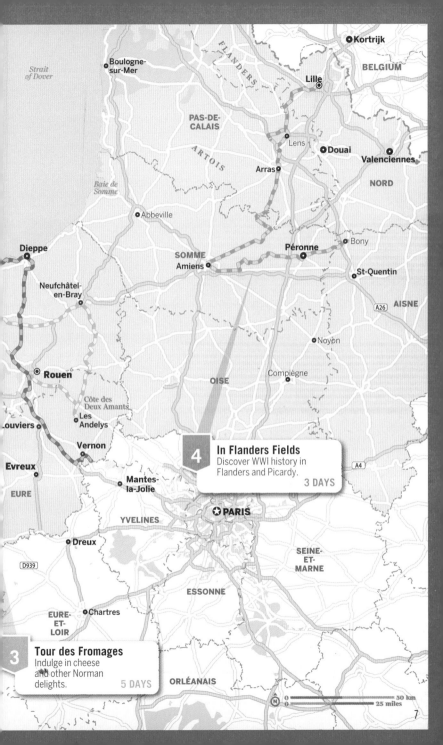

Strait
of Dover

Boulogne-
sur-Mer

⊙Kortrijk

BELGIUM

Lille

FLANDERS

**PAS-DE-
CALAIS**

ARTOIS

Lens

⊙Douai

Valenciennes

Arras⊙

NORD

Baie de
Somme

⊙Abbeville

SOMME

Amiens ⊙

Péronne

⊙ Bony

⊙St-Quentin

Dieppe

Neufchâtel-
en-Bray

AISNE

A26

⊙ Noyon

⊙ Rouen

Côte des
Deux Amants

Compiègne
⊙

OISE

Louviers ⊙

⊙Les
Andelys

Vernon

Evreux

EURE

**Mantes-
la-Jolie**

A4

4 **In Flanders Fields**
Discover WWI history in
Flanders and Picardy.
3 DAYS

✪ PARIS

YVELINES

⊙ Dreux

**SEINE-
ET-
MARNE**

D939

ESSONNE

**EURE-
ET-
LOIR**

⊙Chartres

3 **Tour des Fromages**
Indulge in cheese
and other Norman
delights.   5 DAYS

ORLÉANAIS

0 ————————— 50 km
0 ————————— 25 miles

N

7

Vimy Ridge (left) Walk through one of the only surviving trench systems from WWI. See it on Trip 4

Camembert (above) Learn about the eponymous soft cheese in this picturesque Norman village. See it on Trip 3

Omaha Beach (right) Remember the fallen at the site of the most brutal of the D-Day fighting. See it on Trip 1

Basilique du Sacré-Cœur, Paris

PARIS

If ever a city needed no introduction, it's Paris – a trendsetter and style icon for centuries, and still at the cutting edge. Whether you want tick off the landmarks or seek out secret corners, Paris fulfils all your expectations and leaves you wanting more.

Getting Around

Driving in Paris is a nightmare. Happily, there's no need for a car. The metro is fast, frequent and efficient; tickets cost €1.90 and are valid on the city's buses.

Paris is increasingly bike-friendly, with more cycling lanes and efforts from the city of Paris to reduce the number of cars on the roads.

Most bike rental places will require a deposit (usually €150 for a standard bike, €300 for electric bikes). Take ID and your bank or credit card.

Freescoot (www.freescoot.fr)

Gepetto et Vélos (www.gepetto-velos.com)

Paris à Vélo, C'est Sympa (www.parisvelosympa.fr)

Parking

Parking meters in Paris do not accept coins; they require a European-compatible chip-enabled credit card.

Municipal public car parks, of which there are more than 200 in Paris, charge between €2 and €6 per hour or €20 to €36 per 24 hours (cash and compatible credit cards accepted). Most are open 24 hours.

Where to Eat

Le Marais is one of the best areas for eating out, with its small restaurants and trendy bistros. Don't miss Paris' street markets: Marché Bastille, rue Montorgueil and rue Mouffetard are full of atmosphere.

Where to Stay

Base yourself in Montmartre for its Parisian charm, if you don't mind crowds. Le Marais and Bastille provide style on a budget, while St-Germain is good for a splurge.

Useful Websites

Lonely Planet (www.lonelyplanet.com/paris) Destination information, hotel bookings, traveller forum and more.

Paris Info (www.parisinfo.com) Comprehensive tourist-authority website.

Sortiraparis (www.sortiraparis.com) Up-to-date calendar listing.

Bonjour Paris (www.bonjourparis.com) New openings, old favourites and upcoming events.

HiP Paris (www.hipparis.com) Not only vacation rentals but articles and reviews, too.

Bar, Vieux Lille (Old Lille)

LILLE

Lille may be France's most underrated major city. This once-tired industrial metropolis has transformed itself into a stylish, self-confident city. Three art museums, lots of stylish shops and a lovely old town make it well worthy of investigation.

Getting Around

Driving into Lille is incredibly confusing, even with a good map; just suspend your sense of direction and blindly follow the 'Centre Ville' signs.

Public transport tickets (€1.60, plus €0.20 for a reusable ticket) are sold on buses but must be purchased before boarding a metro or tram; there are ticket machines at each stop. A Pass' Journée (24-hour pass) costs €4.80 and needs to be time-stamped each time you board; two- to seven-day passes are also available. A Pass Soirée, good for unlimited travel after 7pm, costs €2.20.

Transpole has a **ticket office** (📞03 20 40 40 40; www. transpole.fr; Gare Lille-Flandres; ⏰6.30am-8pm Mon-Fri, 9am-8pm Sat; Ⓜ Gare Lille-Flandres)

adjacent to the Gare Lille-Flandres metro station.

Parking

If you're driving, the best idea is to leave your vehicle at the park-and-ride at Champ de Mars on bd de la Liberté, 1.2km northwest of the centre. The ticket includes return travel for five people to central Lille on bus 12.

Where to Eat

The city has a flourishing culinary scene. Keep an eye out for *estaminets* (traditional Flemish eateries, with antique knick-knacks on the walls and plain wooden tables) serving Flemish specialities. Dining hot spots in Vieux Lille include rue de Gand, home to small, moderately priced

French and Flemish restaurants, and rue de la Monnaie and its side streets, alleys and courtyards.

Where to Stay

Most hotels are within striking distance of the city centre, but Lille's business focus means many are short on charm. On the plus side, rates drop at weekends.

Useful Websites

Lille Tourisme (www. lilletourism.com)

Trip Through Lille:

Destination coverage: p80

NEED ^{TO} KNOW

CURRENCY
Euro (€)

LANGUAGE
French

VISAS
Generally not required for stays of up to 90 days (or at all for EU nationals); some nationalities need a Schengen visa.

FUEL
Petrol stations are common around main roads and larger towns. Unleaded costs from around €1.60 per litre; *gazole* (diesel) is usually at least €0.15 cheaper.

RENTAL CARS
ADA (www.ada.fr)

Auto Europe (www.autoeurope.com)

Avis (www.avis.com)

Europcar (www.europcar.com)

Hertz (www.hertz.com)

IMPORTANT NUMBERS
Europe-wide emergency ☏112

Ambulance (SAMU) ☏15

Police ☏17

Climate

Brittany & Normandy •
GO Apr–Sep

• **Paris**
• GO May & Jun

•**French Alps**
GO late Dec–early Apr (skiing) or Jun & Jul (hiking)

French Riviera •
GO Apr–Jun, Sep & Oct

Corsica •
GO Apr–Jun, Sep & Oct

■ Warm to hot summers, mild winters
■ Warm to hot summers, cold winters
■ Mild year-round
■ Mild summers, cold winters
■ Alpine climate

When to Go

High Season (Jun–Aug)
» Médiévales de Bayeux celebrates the city's glorious history with medieval re-enactments in July.

» Queues at big sights and on the road, especially August.

» Book accommodation and tables in the best restaurants well in advance.

Shoulder (Apr–Jun & Sep)
» D-Day commemorations are held on the landing beaches. 2019 sees the 75th anniversary of the epic landings.

» The Deauville American Film Festival is the accessible cousin of Cannes.

» Spring brings warm weather, flowers and local produce.

Low Season (Oct–Mar)
» Prices up to 50% lower than high season.

» Sights, attractions and restaurants open fewer days and shorter hours.

Daily Costs

Budget: Less than €130

» Dorm bed: €18–30

» Double room in budget hotel: €90

» Admission to many attractions first Sunday of month: free

» Lunch *menus* (set meals): less than €20

Midrange: €130–220

» Double room in a midrange hotel: €90–190

» Lunch *menus* in gourmet restaurants: €20–40

Top end: More than €220

» Double room in a top-end hotel: €190–350

» Top restaurant dinner: *menu* €65, à la carte €100–150

» Opera tickets: €15–150

Eating

In cities there are a multitude of places to eat. To dine fine and eat local, book ahead, particularly for weekend dining.

Restaurants and bistros Range from unchanged for a century to contemporary minimalist.

Brasseries Open from dawn until late, these casual eateries are great for dining in between standard meal times.

Cafes Ideal for breakfast and light lunch; many morph into bars after dark.

Sleeping

Be it a fairy-tale château, a boutique hideaway or floating pod on a lake, Normandy has accommodation to suit every taste and pocket. If you're visiting in high season (especially August), reserve ahead.

B&Bs Enchanting properties with maximum five rooms.

Camping Sites range from wild and remote, to brash resorts with pools, slides et al.

Hostels New-wave hostels are design-driven, lifestyle spaces with single/double rooms as well as dorms.

Hotels Hotels embrace every budget and taste.

Arriving in Normandy

Ferry

Car ferries link Dieppe with the English port of Newhaven; Le Havre and Ouistreham (Caen) with Portsmouth; and Cherbourg with Poole and Portsmouth as well as the Irish ports of Dublin and Rosslare.

Train

Normandy is easily accessible by train from Paris – Rouen is just 70 minutes from Paris' Gare St-Lazare (€24.10, 1¼ hours, 25 daily Monday to Friday, 13 to 18 Saturday and Sunday).

Bus

Bus Verts (☎09 70 83 00 14; www.busverts.fr) runs buses from Le Havre to Honfleur (€4.90, 30 minutes, four to six daily) and Deauville and Trouville (€4.90, one hour, four to six daily).

Mobile Phones

European and Australian phones work, but American cells with 900 and 1800 MHz networks only are compatible; check with your provider before leaving home.

Use a French SIM card to call with a cheaper French number.

Internet Access

Wi-fi is available in most hotels and B&Bs (usually free, but sometimes for a small charge). Many cafes and restaurants also offer free wi-fi to customers.

Money

ATMs are at every airport, most train stations and on every second street corner in towns and cities. Visa, MasterCard and Amex are widely accepted.

Tipping

By law, restaurant and bar prices are *service compris* (include a 15% service charge). Taxis expect around 10%; round up bar bills to the nearest euro.

Useful Websites

Tourism Normandie (www.normandie-tourisme.fr) Official regional tourism site.

Apples, Cider and Calvados (vimoutiers.net/AppleCiderCalvados.htm) Normandy's famous apples and its fine apple-centric produce.

Fromages AOP de Normandie (www.fromage-normandie.com) Feeling cheesy?

Lonely Planet (www.lonelyplanet.com) Destination information, hotel bookings, traveller forum and more.

For more, see France Driving Guide (p101).

Road Trips

Les Andelys (p39) on the Seine
LEONID ANDRONOV/SHUTTERSTOCK ©

D-Day's Beaches

1

Explore the events of D-Day, when Allied troops stormed ashore to liberate Europe from Nazi occupation. From war museums to landing beaches, it's a fascinating and sobering experience.

TRIP HIGHLIGHTS

88 km

Omaha Beach
Pay your respects at the Normandy American Cemetery & Memorial

Utah Beach
FINISH

8

7

Carentan

Isigny-sur-Mer

Sully

1

START

Pointe du Hoc
Wander among shell craters that haven't changed since D-Day

98 km

Caen
Visit an award-winning multimedia D-Day museum

0 km

3 DAYS
142KM / 88 MILES

GREAT FOR...

BEST TIME TO GO
April to July, to avoid summer-holiday traffic around the beaches.

ESSENTIAL PHOTO
The forest of white marble crosses at the Normandy American Cemetery & Memorial.

BEST FOR HISTORY
Le Mémorial – Un Musée pour la Paix provides you with a comprehensive D-Day overview.

1 D-Day's Beaches

The beaches and bluffs are quiet today, but on 6 June 1944 the Normandy shoreline witnessed the arrival of the largest armada the world has ever seen. This patch of the French coast will forever be synonymous with D-Day (known to the French as Jour-J), and the coastline is strewn with memorials, museums and cemeteries – reminders that though victory was won on the Longest Day, it came at a terrible price.

TRIP HIGHLIGHT

❶ Caen (p69)

Situated 3km northwest of Caen, the award-winning **Le Mémorial – Un Musée pour la Paix** (Memorial – A Museum for Peace; ☎02 31 06 06 44; www.memorial-caen.fr; esplanade Général Eisenhower; adult/child €19.80/17.50, family pass €51; ☺9am-7pm Apr-Sep, 9.30am-6pm Oct-Dec, 9am-6pm Feb-Mar, closed 3 weeks in Jan, shut most Mon in Nov & Dec) is a brilliant place to begin with some background on the historic events of D-Day, and the wider

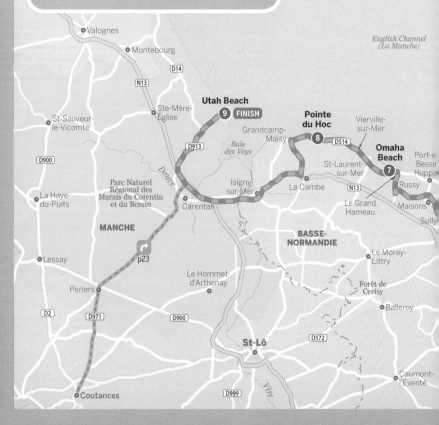

context of WWII. Housed in a purpose-designed building covering 14,000 sq metres, the memorial offers an immersive experience, using sound, lighting, film, animation and audio testimony to evoke the grim realities of war, the trials of occupation and the joy of liberation.

The visit begins with a whistle-stop overview of Europe's descent into total war, tracing events from the end of WWI through to the rise of fascism in Europe, the German occupation of France and the Battle of Normandy. A second section focuses on the Cold War. There's also a well-preserved original bunker used by German command in 1944.

On your way around, look out for a Hawker Typhoon fighter plane and a full-size Sherman tank.

The Drive » From the museum, head northeast along Esplanade Brillaud de Laujardière, and follow signs to Ouistreham. You'll join the E46 ring road; follow it to exit 3a (Porte d'Angleterre), and merge onto the D515, D514 and D84 to Ouistreham. Park on the seafront on bd Aristide Briand. In all it's a trip of 18km.

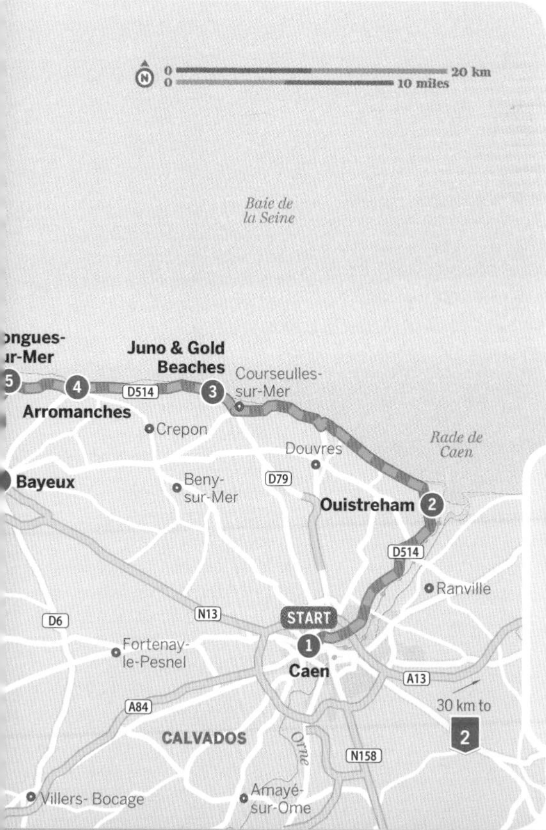

❷ Ouistreham

On D-Day, the sandy seafront around Ouistreham was code named **Sword Beach** and was the focus of attack for the British 3rd Infantry Division.

There are precious few reminders of the battle now, but on D-Day the scene was very different: most of the surrounding buildings had been levelled by artillery fire, and German bunkers and artillery positions were strung out along the seafront. Sword Beach was the site of some of the most famous images of D-Day – including the infamous ones of British troops landing with bicycles, and bagpiper Bill Millin piping troops ashore while under heavy fire.

The Drive » Follow the seafront west onto rue de Lion, following signs for 'Overlord – L'Assaut' onto the D514 towards Courseulles-sur-Mer, 18km west. Drive through town onto rue de Ver, and follow signs to 'Centre Juno Beach'.

NORMANDY & D-DAY BEACHES **1** D-DAY'S BEACHES

Baie de la Seine

0 — 20 km
0 — 10 miles

Longues-sur-Mer ⑤ ④ [D514] ③ Courseulles-sur-Mer
Juno & Gold Beaches
Arromanches
● Crepon
Bayeux ● Beny-sur-Mer [D79]
Douvres
Ouistreham ❷
Rade de Caen
[D514]
● Ranville
[D6] [N13] **START** ❶ **Caen**
Fortenay-le-Pesnel
[A13]
30 km to
● Villers-Bocage [A84] **CALVADOS** Amayé-sur-Ome [N158] ❷

LINK YOUR TRIP

❷ Monet's Normandy
From the end of our Monet-themed trip at Fécamp, drive southwest on the A29 and A13 to Caen, a journey of just under 130km.

19

③ Juno & Gold Beaches (p69)

On D-Day, Courseulles-sur-Mer was known as Juno Beach, and was stormed mainly by Canadian troops. It was here that the exiled French General Charles de Gaulle came ashore after the landings – the first 'official' French soldier to set foot in mainland Europe since 1940. He was followed by Winston Churchill on 12 June and King George VI on 16 June. A Cross of Lorraine marks the historic spot.

The area's only Canadian museum, the **Juno Beach Centre** (☏02 31 37 32 17; www.junobeach. org; voie des Français Libres, Courseulles-sur-Mer; adult/ child €7/5.50, incl guided tour of Juno Beach €11/9, temporary exhibit only €3; ☀9.30am-7pm Apr-Sep, 10am-6pm Oct & Mar, 10am-5pm Nov-Dec & Feb, closed Jan) **has exhibits on Canada's role in the war effort and the landings, and offers guided tours of Juno Beach, including

LUIS FCO. PIZARRO RUIZ/SHUTTERSTOCK ©

the bunker there, from April to October. A short way west is Gold Beach, attacked by the British 50th Infantry on D-Day.

The Drive ⟫ Drive west along the D514 for 14km to Arromanches. You'll pass a car park and viewpoint marked with a statue of the Virgin Mary, which overlooks Port Winston and Gold Beach. Follow the road into town and signs to Musée du Débarquement.

④ Arromanches (p68)

This seaside town was the site of one of the great logistical achievements of D-Day. In order to unload the vast quantities of cargo needed by the invasion forces without capturing one of the heavily defended Channel ports, the Allies set up prefabricated marinas

D-DAY DRIVING ROUTES

There are several signposted driving routes around the main battle sites – look for signs for 'D-Day-Le Choc' in the American sectors and 'Overlord – L'Assaut' in the British and Canadian sectors. A free booklet called *The D-Day Landings & the Battle of Normandy,* available from tourist offices, has details on the eight main routes.

Maps of the D-Day beaches are available at *tabacs* (tobacconists), newsagents and bookshops in Bayeux and elsewhere.

Mulberry Harbour, Arromanches

off two landing beaches, code named **Mulberry Harbour**. These consisted of 146 massive cement caissons towed over from England and sunk to form a semicircular breakwater in which floating bridge spans were moored. In the three months after D-Day, the Mulberries facilitated the unloading of a mind-boggling 2.5 million men, four million tonnes of equipment and 500,000 vehicles.

At low tide, the stanchions of one of these artificial quays, **Port Winston** (named after Winston Churchill), can still be seen on the sands at Arromanches.

Beside the beach, the **Musée du Débarquement** (Landing Museum; ☎02 31 22 34 31; www.musee-arromanches.fr; place du 6 Juin; adult/child €8/5.90; ☺9am-12.30pm & 1.30-6pm Apr-Sep, 10am-12.30pm & 1.30-5pm Oct-Dec, Feb & Mar, closed Jan) explains the logistics and importance of Port Winston; the museum has been expanded for the 75th anniversary of D-Day in 2019.

The Drive » Continue west along the D514 for 6km to the village of Longues-sur-Mer. You'll see the sign for the Batterie de Longues on your right.

⑤ Longues-sur-Mer (p69)

At Longues-sur-Mer you can get a glimpse of the awesome firepower available to the German defenders in the shape of a row of 150mm artillery guns, still housed in their concrete casements. On D-Day they were capable of hitting targets over 20km away – including Gold Beach (to the east) and Omaha Beach (to the west). Parts of the classic D-Day film *The Longest Day* (1962) were filmed here.

The Drive » Backtrack to the crossroads and head straight over onto the D104, signed to Vaux-sur-Aure/Bayeux, for 8km. When you reach town, turn right onto the D613, and follow signs to the 'Musée de la Bataille de Normandie'.

❻ Bayeux (p62)

Though best known for its medieval tapestry, Bayeux has another claim to fame: it was the first town to be liberated after D-Day (on the morning of 7 June 1944).

It's also home to the largest of Normandy's 18 Commonwealth military cemeteries – the **Bayeux War Cemetery**, situated on bd Fabien Ware. It

contains 4848 graves of soldiers from the UK and 10 other countries – including Germany. Across the road is a memorial for 1807 Commonwealth soldiers whose remains were never found. The Latin inscription reads: 'We, whom William once conquered, have now set free the conqueror's native land'.

Nearby, the **Musée Mémorial de la Bataille de Normandie** (Battle of Normandy Memorial Museum; ☎02 31 51 46 90; www.bayeuxmuseum.com; bd Fabien Ware; adult/child €7.50/5; ☺9.30am-6.30pm May-Sep, 10am-12.30pm & 2-6pm Oct-Apr, closed 3 weeks in Jan) explores

the battle through photos, personal accounts, dioramas and film.

The Drive » After overnighting in Bayeux, head northwest of town on the D6 towards Port-en-Bessin-Huppain. You'll reach a Super-U supermarket after about 10km. Go round the roundabout and turn onto the D514 for another 8km. You'll see signs to the 'Cimetière Americain' near the hamlet of Le Bray. Omaha Beach is another 4km further on, near Vierville-sur-Mer.

TRIP HIGHLIGHT

❼ Omaha Beach (p68)

If anywhere symbolises the courage and sacrifice of D-Day, it's Omaha – still known as 'Bloody Omaha' to US veterans. It was here, on the 7km stretch of coastline between Vierville-sur-Mer, St-Laurent-sur-Mer and Colleville-sur-Mer, that the most brutal fighting on D-Day took place. US troops had to fight their way across the beach towards the heavily defended cliffs, exposed to underwater obstacles, hidden minefields and withering crossfire. The toll was heavy: of the 2500 casualties at Omaha on D-Day, more than 1000 were fatal; most of those killed died within the first hour of the landings.

High on the bluffs above Omaha, the **Normandy American Cemetery & Memorial** (☎02

D-DAY IN FIGURES

Code named 'Operation Overlord', the D-Day landings were the largest military operation in history. On the morning of 6 June 1944, swarms of landing craft – part of an armada of over 6000 ships and 13,000 aeroplanes – hit the northern Normandy beaches, and tens of thousands of soldiers from the USA, the UK, Canada and elsewhere began pouring onto French soil. The initial landing force involved some 45,000 troops; 15 more divisions were to follow once successful beachheads had been established.

The majority of the 135,000 Allied troops stormed ashore along 80km of beaches north of Bayeux code named (from west to east) Utah, Omaha, Gold, Juno and Sword. The landings were followed by the 76-day Battle of Normandy, during which the Allies suffered 210,000 casualties, including 37,000 troops killed. German casualties are believed to have been around 200,000; another 200,000 German soldiers were taken prisoner. About 14,000 French civilians also died.

For more background and statistics, see www.normandie44lamemoire.com, www.dday-overlord.com and www.6juin1944.com.

31 51 62 00; www.abmc.gov; Colleville-sur-Mer; ⏰9am-6pm mid-Apr–mid-Sep, to 5pm mid-Sep–mid-Apr) provides a sobering reminder of the human cost of the battle. Featured in the opening scenes of *Saving Private Ryan*, this is the largest American cemetery in Europe, containing the graves of 9387 American soldiers, and a memorial to 1557 comrades 'known only unto God'.

Start off in the very thoughtfully designed visitor centre, which has moving portrayals of some of the soldiers buried here. Afterwards, take in the expanse of white marble crosses and Stars of David that stretch off in seemingly endless rows, surrounded by an immaculately tended expanse of lawn.

The Drive ›› From the Vierville-sur-Mer seafront, follow the rural D514 through quiet countryside towards Grandcamp-Maisy. After about 10km you'll see signs to 'Pointe du Hoc'.

- - - - - - - - - - - - - - - - - -

TRIP HIGHLIGHT

❽ Pointe du Hoc

West of Omaha, this craggy promontory was the site of D-Day's most audacious military exploit. At 7.10am, 225 US Army Rangers command-ed by Lt Col James Earl Rudder scaled the sheer 30m cliffs, where the Germans had stationed a battery of artillery guns trained onto the beaches

DETOUR: COUTANCES

Start: ❾ Utah Beach

The lovely old Norman town of Coutances makes a good detour when travelling between the D-Day beaches and Mont St-Michel. At the town's heart is its Gothic **Cathédrale Notre-Dame de Coutances** (http://cathedralecoutances.free.fr; parvis Notre-Dame; ⏰8.30am-noon & 2-5.30pm). Interior highlights include several 13th-century windows, a 14th-century fresco of St Michael skewering the dragon, and an organ and high altar from the mid-1700s. You can climb the lantern tower on a tour (adult/child €8/4). Coutances is about 50km south of Utah Beach by the most direct route.

- - - - - - - - - - - - - - - - - -

of Utah and Omaha. Unfortunately, the guns had already been moved inland, and Rudder and his men spent the next two days repelling counterattacks. By the time they were finally relieved on 8 June, 81 of the rangers had been killed and 58 more had been wounded.

Today the **site** (☎02 31 51 90 70; www.abmc.gov; ⏰9am-6pm mid-Apr–mid-Sep, to 5pm rest of year), which France turned over to the US government in 1979, looks much as it did on D-Day, com-plete with shell craters and crumbling gun emplacements.

The Drive ›› Stay on the D514 to Grandcamp-Maisy, then continue south onto the D13 dual carriageway. Stay on the road till you reach the turn-off for the D913, signed to St-Marie-du-Mont/Utah Beach. It's a drive of 44km.

❾ Utah Beach

The D-Day tour ends at St-Marie-du-Mont, aka Utah Beach, assaulted by soldiers of the US 4th and 8th Infantry Divisions. The beach was relatively lightly defended, and by midday the landing force had linked with para-troopers from the 101st Airborne. By nightfall, some 20,000 men and 1700 vehicles had arrived on French soil, and the road to European libera-tion had begun.

Today the site is marked by military me-morials and the **Musée du Débarquement** (Utah Beach Landing Museum; ☎02 33 71 53 35; www.utah-beach.com; Ste-Marie du Mont; adult/child €8/4; ⏰9.30am-7pm Jun-Sep, 10am-6pm Oct-May, closed Jan) inside the former German com-mand post.

Monet's Normandy

This eclectic trip takes art lovers on a fascinating spin around eastern Normandy. En route you'll hit the key landscapes and cities that inspired Monet, the father of impressionism.

2

TRIP HIGHLIGHTS

190 km

Étretat
Phenomenal views of the dramatic coastline

Dieppe

St-Valery-en-Caux

6 **Fécamp**

Le Havre

8

Deauville & Trouville-sur-Mer **FINISH**

2

70 km

Rouen
Museums and a magnificent cathedral

1 **START**

Honfleur
A wonderfully picturesque harbour town

235 km

Giverny
The cradle of impressionism

0 km

---

4 DAYS
290KM / 180 MILES

GREAT FOR...

BEST TIME TO GO

Any time from September to June for perfectly nuanced light.

ESSENTIAL PHOTO

Snap the truly extraordinary coastal vista from the clifftop in Étretat.

BEST FOR CULTURE

Rouen has plenty of top-quality museums and historic buildings.

Giverny Water garden, Maison et Jardins de Claude Monet (p26)

25

2 Monet's Normandy

Be prepared for a visual feast on this four-day trip around the eastern part of Normandy – the cradle of impressionism. Starting from the village of Giverny, location of the most celebrated garden in France, you'll follow in the footsteps of Monet and other impressionist megastars, taking in medieval Rouen, the dramatic Côte d'Albâtre, Le Havre, Honfleur and Trouville-sur-Mer. This is your chance to see first-hand why so many painters were attracted to this place.

TRIP HIGHLIGHT

❶ Giverny

The tiny country village of Giverny is a place of pilgrimage for devotees of impressionism. Monet lived here from 1883 until his death in 1926, in a rambling house surrounded by flower-filled gardens. It's now the immensely popular **Maison et Jardins de Claude Monet** (☎02 32 51 28 21; www.fondation-monet. com; 84 rue Claude Monet; adult/child €9.50/5.50, incl Musée des Impressionnismes

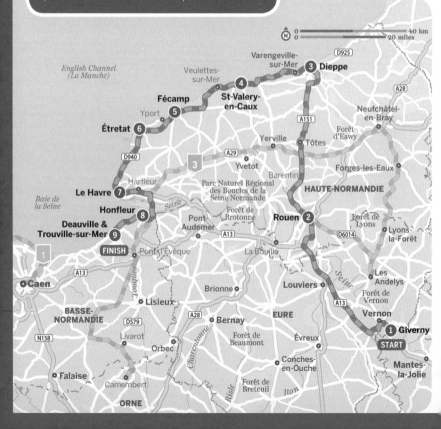

Giverny €17/9; ⏱9.30am-6pm Easter-Oct). His pastel-pink house and Water Lily studio stand on the periphery of the garden (called 'Clos Normand'), and the symmetrically laid-out gardens burst with flowers.

The Drive » It's a 70km trip (one hour) to Rouen. Head to Vernon and follow signs to Rouen along the A13. A more scenic (but longer) route is via Les Andelys, along the east bank of the Seine.

- - - - - - - - - - - - - - - - -

TRIP HIGHLIGHT

❷ Rouen (p51)

With its elegant spires and atmospheric medieval quarter complete with narrow lanes and wonky half-timbered houses, it's no wonder that Rouen has inspired numerous painters,

LINK YOUR TRIP

Tour des Fromages

From Honfleur or Rouen you can embark on a gastronomic drive, and taste and learn about some of the best cheese in France at various cheese museums.

D-Day's Beaches

From Trouville-sur-Mer, it's an easy 50km drive west to Caen, the obvious starting point for the D-Day beaches.

including Monet. Some of his works, including one of his studies of the stunning Gothic cathedral (p51), are displayed at the splendid Musée des Beaux-Arts (p51). Feeling inspired? Sign up for an art class with the tourist office (p55) and create your own Rouen Cathedral canvas from the very room in which Monet painted his series of that building.

If you're at all interested in architectural glories, the 14th-century Abbatiale St-Ouen (p53), which is a marvellous example of the Rayonnant Gothic style, is a must-see abbey. There's also much Joan of Arc lore in Rouen (she was executed here in 1431). For the story of her life don't miss the spectacular audio-visual displays in the Historial Jeanne d'Arc (p51).

The Drive » Follow signs to Dieppe. Count on 45 minutes for the 65km trip.

- - - - - - - - - - - - - - - - -

❸ Dieppe (p55)

Sandwiched between limestone cliffs, Dieppe is a small-scale fishing port with a pleasant seafront promenade. Still used by fishing vessels but dominated by pleasure craft, the **port** makes for a bracing sea-air stroll. High above the city on the western cliff, the 15th-century Château-Musée (p55) is the town's

most imposing landmark. Monet immortalised **Pourville**, a seaside village on the western outskirts of Dieppe.

The Drive » Take the scenic coastal roads (D75 and D68), rather than the inland D925, via the resort towns of Pourville, Varengeville-sur-Mer, Quiberville, St-Aubin-sur-Mer, Sotteville-sur-Mer and Veules-les-Roses (35km, 45 minutes).

- - - - - - - - - - - - - - - - -

❹ St-Valery-en-Caux (p57)

You're now in the heart of the scenic Côte d'Albâtre (Alabaster Coast), which stretches from Dieppe southwest to Étretat. With its lofty bone-white cliffs, this wedge of coast is a geological wonder world that charmed a generation of impressionists, including Monet. Once you get a glimpse of sweet little St-Valery-en-Caux, with its delightful port, lovely stretch of stony beach and majestic cliffs, you'll see why.

The Drive » Take the coastal road (D79) via Veulettes-sur-Mer. Count on an hour for the 36km trip.

- - - - - - - - - - - - - - - - -

❺ Fécamp (p58)

After all that driving along the Côte d'Albâtre, it's time to stop for a glass of Bénédictine at the **Palais de la Bénédictine** (☎02 35 10 26 10; www.benedictinedom.com; 110 rue Alexandre Le Grand; adult/child €12/7, guided tour adult/

child €18/10; ⊙ ticket sales 10.30-11.30am & 2.30-4.30pm mid-Dec–mid-Apr, longer hours mid-Apr–mid-Dec, closed early Jan–mid-Feb). Opened in 1900, this unusually ornate factory is where all the Bénédictine liqueur in the world is made.

Be sure to drive up north to **Cap Fagnet** (110m), which offers gobsmacking views of the town and the coastline.

The Drive » Follow signs to Étretat (17km, along the D940). You could also start on the D940 and turn off onto the more scenic D11 (via Yport).

TRIP HIGHLIGHT

⑥ Étretat (p59)

Is Étretat the most enticing town in Normandy? It's picture-postcard everywhere you look. The dramatic white cliffs that bookend the town, the Falaise d'Aval (p59) to the southwest and the Falaise d'Amont (p59) to the northeast, will stick in your memory. Once at the top, you'll pinch yourself to see if it's real – the views are sensational. Such irresistible scenery

CLAUDE MONET

The undisputed leader of the impressionists, Claude Monet was born in Paris in 1840 and grew up in Le Havre, where he found an early affinity with the outdoors.

From 1867 Monet's distinctive style began to emerge, focusing on the effects of light and colour and using the quick, undisguised broken brushstrokes that would characterise the impressionist period. His contemporaries were Pissarro, Renoir, Sisley, Cézanne and Degas. The young painters left the studio to work outdoors, experimenting with the shades and hues of nature, and arguing and sharing ideas. Their work was far from welcomed by critics; one of them condemned it as 'impressionism', in reference to Monet's *Impression: Sunrise* when exhibited in 1874.

From the late 1870s Monet concentrated on painting in series, seeking to recreate a landscape by showing its transformation under different conditions of light and atmosphere. In 1883 Monet moved to Giverny, planting his property with a variety of flowers around an artificial pond, the Jardin d'Eau, in order to paint the subtle effects of sunlight on natural forms. It was here that he painted the *Nymphéas* (Water Lilies) series.

For more info on Monet and his work, visit www.giverny.org.

Cathédrale Notre Dame, Rouen (p27)

HUANG ZHENG/SHUTTERSTOCK ©

made Étretat a favourite of painters, especially Monet, who produced more than 80 canvases of the scenery here.

The Drive » Follow signs to Le Havre (28km, along the D940 and the D147). Count on about half an hour for the journey.

❼ Le Havre (p59)

It was in Le Havre that Monet painted the defining impressionist view. His 1873 canvas of the harbour at dawn was entitled *Impression: Sunrise*. Monet wouldn't recognise present-day Le Havre: all but obliterated in September 1944 by Allied bomb-

ing raids, the city centre was totally redesigned after the war by Belgian architect Auguste Perret. Make sure you visit the **Musée Malraux** (MuMa; ☎02 35 19 62 62; www.muma-lehavre.fr/en; 2 bd Clemenceau; adult/under 26yr €7/free; ⊙11am-6pm Tue-Fri, to 7pm Sat & Sun), which houses a truly fabulous collection of impressionist works, with canvases by Claude Monet, Eugène Boudin, Camille Corot and many more. Then take in the Église St-Joseph (p60), a modern church whose interior is a luminous work of art – thanks to 13,000 panels of coloured glass

on its walls and tower. For doses of Baroque ecclesiastical architecture, stop by Cathédrale Notre-Dame (p60).

The Drive » Follow signs to Pont de Normandie, which links Le Havre to Honfleur (toll €5.40).

- - - - - - - - - - - - - - - - -

TRIP HIGHLIGHT

❽ Honfleur (p75)

Honfleur is exquisite to look at. (No, you're not dreaming!) Its heart is the highly picturesque **Vieux Bassin** (Old Harbour), from where explorers once set sail for the New World. Marvel at the extraordinary 15th-century wooden Église

Falaise d'Aval, Étretat (p28)

Ste-Catherine (p38), complete with a roof that from the inside resembles an upturned boat, then wander the warren of flower-filled cobbled streets lined with wooden and stone buildings.

Honfleur's graceful beauty has inspired numerous painters, including Eugène Boudin, an early impressionist painter born here in 1824, and Monet. Their works are displayed at the Musée Eugène Boudin (p76). Honfleur was also the birthplace of composer Erik Satie. The fascinating Les Maisons Satie (p76) is packed with sur-realist surprises, all set to his ethereal compositions.

The Drive >> From Honfleur it's a 14km trip to Trouville-sur-Mer along the D513 (about 20 minutes).

----

⑨ Deauville (p72) & Trouville-sur-Mer (p74)

Finish your impressionist road trip in style by heading southwest to the twin seaside resorts of Deauville and Trouville-sur-Mer, which are only separated by a river bridge but maintain distinctly different personalities. Exclusive, expensive and brash, Deauville is packed with designer boutiques, deluxe hotels and public gardens of impossible neatness, and is home to two racetracks and a high-profile American film festival.

Trouville-sur-Mer, another veteran beach resort, is more down to earth. During the 19th century the town was frequented by writers and painters, including Monet, who spent his honeymoon here in 1870. No doubt he was lured by the picturesque port, the 2km-long sandy beach lined with opulent villas, and the laid-back ambience.

Tour des Fromages

On this gastronomic drive you'll devour some of the best cheese in France and see where the seaside inspired artists, where Joan of Arc was executed and where Richard the Lionheart prowled.

3

TRIP HIGHLIGHTS

70 km

Honfleur
Savour superfresh seafood at the harbourside restaurants

315 km

Rouen
Admire the architecture of Rouen's old town

Neufchâtel-en-Bray

8

11 **FINISH**

● **Pont-l'Évêque**

Les Andelys

3

15 km

START **1**

Livarot
Explore the best cheese museum in France

Camembert
Learn the secrets of the world-renowned cheese at the Président Farm

0 km

5 DAYS
315KM / 196 MILES

GREAT FOR...

BEST TIME TO GO
In May Pont L'Évêque celebrates all that is cheese during the Fête du Fromage.

ESSENTIAL PHOTO

Snap a shot of the Seine through the ruined windows of Château Gaillard.

BEST FOR HISTORY

Pay your respects to the memory of Joan of Arc in Rouen.

French cheeses

33

3 Tour des Fromages

More cheese, please! It's said that in France there is a different variety of cheese for every day of the year. On this driving culinary extravaganza, you'll taste – and learn about – some of the very finest of French cheeses. Cheese cravings sated, explore the backstreets of Rouen, build castles made of sand on the seashore and clamber up to castles made of stone in the interior.

TRIP HIGHLIGHT

❶ Camembert

Thanks to a delicious soft cheese, the name Camembert is known the world over. Therefore, it can come as a surprise to learn that Camembert is merely a small, but very picturesque, classic Norman village of half-timbered buildings. The big attraction here is, of course, its cheese, and you can learn all about it during a guided tour of the **Président Farm** (☎02 33 12 10 37; www.maison

ducamembert.com; adult/child €4/2; ⊕10am-noon & 2-5pm daily May-Sep, Wed-Sun Apr & Oct, closed Nov-late Mar), an early-19th-century farm restored by Président, one of the region's largest Camembert producers.

The Drive ≫ It's a 5km, 10-minute drive along the D246 and then the D16 from Camembert village to the Musée du Camembert in Vimoutiers.

❷ Vimoutiers

Make a stop in the in the village of Vimoutiers to visit the small **Musée du**

Camembert – recently reopened after extensive renovations – which gives you the lowdown on the history and culture of the smelly stuff. It's a privately run affair; you might have to call for them to open up.

The Drive ≫ It's another 10-minute drive north to stop 3, Livarot, along the D579.

- - - - - - - - - - - - - - - -

TRIP HIGHLIGHT

❸ Livarot

Although not as famous internationally as Camembert, Livarot is a big deal in France. The town where the cheese of the same name originated is home to probably the best cheese tour in Normandy. **Le Village Fromager** (L'Atelier Fromager; ☎02 31 48 20 10; www.graindorge.fr; 42 rue du Général Leclerc; ⊕9.30am-5pm Mon-Sat, from 10.30am Sun Jul & Aug, 9.30am-1pm & 2-5.30pm Mon-Sat Apr-Jun, Sep & Oct, shorter hours rest of year) offers a free tour and tasting at the Graindorge factory. A self-guided tour accompanied by multimedia displays

LINK YOUR TRIP

4 **In Flanders Fields**
The war memorials of northern France are a powerful symbol of the wastefulness of war. Amiens, the start of our Flanders Fields drive, is 120km from Rouen.

leads through a series of whiffy viewing rooms where you can watch Livarot, Camembert and Pont l'Évêque being made.

After you've expanded your waistline on the cheese tour, work it all off again with a walk around the town. Its wobbly-wiggly half-timbered buildings make it a real charmer.

The Drive ≫ Head west along the D4 from Livarot to the village of St-Pierre-sur-Dives. The D271 leads to Les Arpents du Soleil winery a little south of the village en route to Grisy.

- - - - - - - - - - - - - - - -

❹ Les Arpents du Soleil

From Livarot, we're detouring a little further west. Just outside the village of St-Pierre-sur-Dives is something of a surprise for Normandy – not a cider farm, but a renowned vineyard, **Les Arpents du Soleil** (☎02 31 40 71 82; www.arpents-du-soleil.com; Chemin des Vignes, Grisy; guided tour adult €7.50; ⊕shop 2-6.30pm Mon & Fri, 10am-5pm 1st Sat of month & each Sat in Dec, tours 2.30pm Thu Apr-Nov). A winemaker since medieval times, the vineyard's current crop includes three dry whites and a fruity, oaky pinot noir. The shop is open year-round, and offers the chance to try the estate's wines, but guided tours only run on certain days, so phone ahead.

SOMME

Amiens

D929

Longueau

A16

NORD-PAS-DE-CALAIS

...auvais

OISE

Forêt d'Halatte   Bray

A16   Forêt d'Ermenonville

Forêt de Chantilly

PARIS

ÎLE DE FRANCE

Versailles

35

The Drive » Retrace your route to St-Pierre-sur-Dives, then head north on the D16 all the way to Crèvecoeur-en-Auge, and follow the road onto the D101 to Les Jardins du Pays d'Auge.

⑤ Les Jardins du Pays d'Auge

A bit further north towards Cambremer is **Les Jardins du Pays d'Auge** (☎06 84 43 59 29; www.lesjardinsdupaysdauge.com; rte des 3 Rois, Cambremer; adult/child €8.10/5; ⊙10am-6.30pm May-Sep, 10am-5pm Mon-Fri 1 Oct-20 Oct; ⍟), a bucolic 4-hectare garden surrounded by typical Norman half-timbered buildings, as well as a museum of old tools. There's also a sweet country cafe where you can try no fewer than 80 crêpes and *galettes*.

The Drive » A gentle countryside cruise of just over half an hour (22km) up the D101 will see you easing into Pont l'Évêque.

⑥ Pont l'Évêque

Since the 13th century this unpretentious little town with rivers meandering through its centre has been known for its eponymous cheese. Although two-thirds of the town was destroyed in WWII, careful reconstruction has brought much of it back to life. Half-timbered buildings line the main street, and 1960s stained glass bathes the 15th-century Église St-Michel in coloured light.

There is no shortage of **cheese shops** in town.

If you're passing through over the sec-

ond weekend in May, don't miss the **Fête du Fromage**, when the townsfolk throw a little party for cheese – only in France!

The Drive » To get to the Distillerie Christian Drouin, your next stop, head out of Pont l'Évêque in a northeasterly direction on the D675. At the roundabout on the edge of the town, take the third exit (rue

---

NORMAN CUISINE

Normandy may be the largest region of France not to make it onto the wine map, but its culinary wealth more than makes up for what it lacks in the wine department – besides, any self-respecting Norman would far rather partake in a locally produced cider or *calvados* (apple-flavoured brandy). This is a land of soft cheeses, apples, cream and an astonishingly rich range of seafood and fish. You simply shouldn't leave Normandy without trying classics such as *coquilles St-Jacques* (scallops) and *sole dieppoise* (Dieppe sole). And whatever you do, don't forget your *trou normand* ('Norman hole') – the traditional break between courses for a glass of *calvados* to cleanse the palate and improve the appetite for the next course!

Honfleur

St-Mélaine/D677) and continue for about 2.5km until you see the farm on your left.

7 Distillerie Christian Drouin

In case you were starting to wonder if Normandy was merely a one-cheese pony, pay a visit to the **Distillerie Christian Drouin** (📞02 31 64 30 05; www.calvados-drouin.com;

rte de Trouville, Coudray-Rabut; 🕙9am-noon & 2-6pm Mon-Sat), which will let you in on the delights of Norman cider and *calvados* (that other classic Norman tipple). Entrance is free.

The Drive » It's a simple enough 17km drive along the D579 to Honfleur and your first sea views (yes, the sun will be out by the time you get there...).

TRIP HIGHLIGHT

8 Honfleur (p75)

Long a favourite with painters, Honfleur is arguably Normandy's most charming seaside town.

On the west side of the Vieux Bassin (p76), with its many pleasure boats, **quai Ste-Catherine** is lined with tall, taper-thin houses – many protected

37

from the elements by slate tiles – dating from the 16th to the 18th centuries. The **Lieutenance**, at the mouth of the old harbour, was once the residence of the town's royal governor.

Initially intended as a temporary structure, the **Église Ste-Catherine** (place Ste-Catherine; ⊙9am-5.15pm or later) has been standing in the square for more than 500 years. The church is particularly notable for its double-vaulted roof and twin naves, which from the inside resemble a couple of overturned ships' hulls.

The Drive » You've had nice, mellow country lanes so far. Time to speed things up

for the 111km race (not too fast, please!) down the A29 to Neufchâtel-en-Bray.

-----

❾ Neufchâtel-en-Bray

The small market town of Neufchâtel-en-Bray is renowned for its heart-shaped cheese called, imaginatively, Neufchâtel. To buy it in the most authentic way, try to time your arrival to coincide with the Saturday-morning **market**.

Appetite satisfied, it's now time for some culture. Check out the **Musée Mathon-Durand** (☎02 35 93 06 55; 53 Grande Rue Saint-Pierre, Neufchâtel-en-Bray; adult/child €4/2; ⊙2-6pm Tue-Sun mid-June–

PAUL TRIDON/GETTY IMAGES ©

mid-Sep, 2-6pm Sat & Sun Apr–mid-June & mid-Sep–Oct), inside a gorgeous medieval building that once belonged to a knight. He's long since gone off to fight dragons in the sky, and today the house contains a small museum of local culture.

The Drive » The most obvious route between Neufchâtel-en-Bray and stop 9, Les Andelys, is along the A28, but that means skirting around Rouen – time it badly and you'll be sitting in traffic breathing in carbon monoxide. Instead, take the more serene D921 back road. Going this way should take you about 80 minutes to cover the 75km.

DETOUR: AMIENS

Start: ❾ Neufchâtel-en-Bray

One of France's most awe-inspiring Gothic cathedrals is reason enough to make a detour to Amiens, the comfy, if reserved, former capital of Picardy. The Cathédrale Notre Dame (p97) is the largest Gothic cathedral in France and a Unesco World Heritage Site. Begun in 1220, the magnificent structure was built to house the **skull of St John the Baptist**, shown – framed in gold and jewels – in the northern outer wall of the ambulatory. Connoisseurs rave about the soaring Gothic arches, the unity of style and the immense interior, but for locals the 17th-century statue known as the **Ange Pleureur** (Crying Angel), in the ambulatory directly behind the over-the-top baroque high altar, remains a favourite.

From Neufchâtel-en-Brey head 73km (one hour) down the A29 toll road and return the same way to Neufchâtel-en-Bray to continue south to Les Andelys.

Les Andelys

🔟 Les Andelys

On a hairpin curve in the Seine lies Les Andelys (the 's' is silent), the old part of which is crowned by the ruins of Château Gaillard, the 12th-century hilltop fastness of Richard the Lionheart.

Built from 1196 to 1197, the noble ruin of **Château Gaillard** (📞02 32 54 41 93; adult/child €3.20/2.70; 🕐10am-1pm & 2-6pm Wed-Mon late Mar-Oct) once secured the western border of English territory along the Seine until Henry IV ordered its destruction in 1603. Fantastic views of the Seine's white cliffs can be enjoyed from the platform a few hundred metres up the one-lane road from the castle.

The Drive ⟫ It's a 45km, 50-minute scamper (well, as long as you don't hit rush-hour traffic) along the D6014 to your final stop, Rouen.

TRIP HIGHLIGHT

🔟 Rouen (p51)

With its elegant spires, beautifully restored medieval quarter and soaring Gothic cathedral, the ancient city of Rouen is one of Normandy's highlights. It was here that the young French heroine Joan of Arc (Jeanne d'Arc) was tried for heresy.

Rouen's stunning Cathédrale Notre Dame (p51) is the famous subject of a series of paintings by Monet.

Rue du Gros Horloge runs from the cathedral west to **place du Vieux Marché**, where you'll find the thrillingly bizarre **Église Jeanne d'Arc** (place du Vieux Marché; 🕐10am-noon & 2-6pm, closed Fri & Sun mornings), with its fish-scale exterior and vast, sublime wall of stained glass. It sits on the spot where the 19-year-old Joan was burned at the stake.

In Flanders Fields

4

WWI history comes to life on this tour of Western Front battlefields, where Allied and German troops endured four years of trench warfare. Lille, Arras and Amiens offer an urban counterpoint.

TRIP HIGHLIGHTS

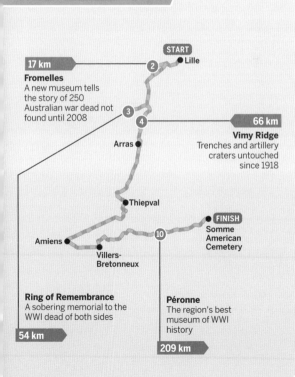

START
● Lille

17 km

Fromelles
A new museum tells the story of 250 Australian war dead not found until 2008

66 km

Vimy Ridge
Trenches and artillery craters untouched since 1918

Arras ●

● Thiepval

FINISH
Somme American Cemetery

Amiens ●

Villers-Bretonneux

Ring of Remembrance
A sobering memorial to the WWI dead of both sides

54 km

Péronne
The region's best museum of WWI history

209 km

3 DAYS
235KM / 146 MILES

GREAT FOR...

BEST TIME TO GO

March to November; a few sites close in December and January.

 ESSENTIAL PHOTO

The staggering list of missing soldiers' names at Thiepval.

 BEST FOR HISTORY

Historial de la Grande Guerre, Péronne's first-rate WWI museum.

In Flanders Fields

Shortly after WWI broke out in 1914, Allied troops established a line of resistance against further German advances in the northern French countryside near Arras, initiating one of the longest and bloodiest standoffs in military history. This tour of Flanders and Picardy takes in some of France's most important WWI battle sites and memorials, along with the charming cities of Lille, Arras and Amiens.

❶ Lille (p80)

A convenient gateway to northern France's WWI battlefields, cosmopolitan Lille offers an engaging mix of grand architecture and Flemish culture. Stop in for dinner at an *estaminet* (traditional Flemish restaurant) and stroll around the bustling pedestrianised centre. Highlights include the **Vieille Bourse** (place du Général de Gaulle; Ⓜ Rihour), a 17th-century Flemish Renaissance extravaganza decorated with caryatids and cornucopia, and the neighbourhood of **Vieux Lille** (Old Lille), where restored 17th- and 18th-century brick houses are home to chic boutiques.

The Drive » Take the westbound A25, the southbound N41, the D207 and finally the D141B to Fromelles, a distance of 17km.

TRIP HIGHLIGHT

❷ Fromelles

The death toll was horrific – 1917 Australians and 519 Britons killed in just one day of fighting – yet the 1916 Battle of Fromelles was largely forgotten until 2008, when the remains of 250 of the fallen were discovered. They are now buried in the Fromelles (Pheasant Wood) Cemetery (p92); 144 have been identified

Aire-sur-la-Lys

[A26]

PAS-DE-CALAIS

St-Pol-sur-Ternoise

Avesnes-le-Comte

La Herlière

[N25]

Doullens

Beauval   Marieux

Puchevillers

[N25]

Contay

[D929]

Somme   Corbie

Amiens ❽   **SOMME**

Longueau   [N29]   ❾

Villers-Bretonneu

250km to Caen

[A16]

Montdidi

Breteuil

OISE

Clermont

thanks to DNA testing. Next door, the excellent Musée de la Bataille de Fromelles (p92) evokes life in the trenches with reconstructed bunkers, photographs and biographies.

The Drive ≫ Take the D22 4km south to the N41, turn southwest and after 3km turn south onto the N47; continue for 12km before turning west onto the A21. Get off at the D937, drive southeast for 5km and then follow the signs to Notre-Dame de Lorette. Total distance: 37km.

TRIP HIGHLIGHT

③ Ring of Remembrance

It's hard not to be overwhelmed by the folly and waste of the Western Front at the **Ring of Remembrance** (L'Anneau de la Mémoire; www.lens14-18.com; chemin du Mont de Lorette, Ablain-St-Nazaire; ⊗8.30am-11pm Apr-Nov, to 8pm Dec-Mar) as you walk past panel after panel engraved with almost 580,000 names: WWI dead from both sides who are listed in strict alphabetical order, without reference to nationality, rank or religion.

The Drive ≫ Return to the D937 and drive south for 6km. Then take the D49 east for 3km, the D917 north for 1km and finally the D55E2 northwest. Total distance: 12.5km

ERIC VALENNE GEOSTORY/SHUTTERSTOCK ©

TRIP HIGHLIGHT

❹ Vimy Ridge

Right after the war, the French attempted to erase all signs of battle and return northern France to agriculture and normalcy. The Canadians took a different approach, deciding that the most evocative way to remember their fallen was to preserve part of the crater-pocked battlefield exactly the way it looked when the guns fell silent. As a result, the best place to get some sense of the hell known as the Western Front is the chilling, eerie moonscape of **Vimy Ridge** (☎03 21 50 68 68; www.cheminsdememoire.gouv. fr; chemins des Canadiens, Vimy; ⊙ memorial site 24hr, visitor centre 10am-6pm May-Oct, 9am-5pm Nov-Apr). During visitor centre opening hours, bilingual Canadian students lead free guided tours of reconstructed tunnels and trenches.

The Drive ≫ Follow the D55E2, N17 and D917 12km into Arras.

❺ Arras (p89)

Contemplating the picture-perfect Flemish-style façades of Arras' two gorgeous market squares, the **Grand' Place** and the **Petite Place** (Place des Héros), it's hard to believe that almost the entire city centre was reduced to rubble during WWI (it was reconstructed in the 1920s). To get a sense of life in wartime Arras, head 1.5km south to **Carrière Wellington** (Wellington Quarry; ☎03 21 51 26 95; www.carrierewellington. com; rue Arthur Delétoille; tours adult/child €7/3.30; ⊙10am-12.30pm & 1.30-6pm, closed Jan), a subterranean quarry that served as a staging area for the Allies' 1917 spring offensive. Prior to the attack, 500 New Zealand soldiers worked round the clock for five months expanding Arras' medieval quarries to accommodate kitchens, a hospital and several thousand Commonwealth troops. Reminders of these events are everywhere, from

Trenches, Vimy Ridge

Maori-language graffiti to candle burn marks from the Easter Mass celebrated underground the day before the troops stormed German front lines.

The Drive » Take the D919, D174 and D73 31km southwest to the Newfoundland Memorial, detouring briefly at kilometre 15 to the Ayette Indian and Chinese Cemetery, a Commonwealth cemetery where Hindi, Arabic and Chinese inscriptions mark the graves of Indian soldiers and Chinese labourers recruited by the British government.

---

⑥ Newfoundland Memorial

On 1 July 1916 the volunteer Royal Newfoundland Regiment stormed entrenched German positions and was nearly wiped out. The evocative Beaumont-Hamel Newfoundland Memorial (p92) preserves the battlefield much as it was at fighting's end. Climb to the bronze caribou statue, on a hillside surrounded by native Newfoundland plants, for views of the shell craters, barbed-wire barriers and zigzag trenches that still fill with mud

DETOUR: CLAIRIÈRE DE L'ARMISTICE

Start: ⑪ **Somme American Cemetery**

On the 11th hour of the 11th day of the 11th month of 1918, WWI officially ended at **Clairière de l'Armistice** (Armistice Clearing), 7km northeast of the city of Compiègne, with the signing of an armistice inside the railway carriage of Allied supreme commander Maréchal Ferdinand Foch. In the same forest clearing, in an almost identical railroad car, the **Musée de l'Armistice** (Armistice Clearing; ☑03 44 85 14 18; www.musee-armistice-14-18.fr; rte de Soissons; adult/child €5/3; ☉10am-6pm Jan-Nov, to 5.30pm Dec) commemorates these events with memorabilia, newspaper clippings and stereoscopic photos that capture – in 3D – all the mud, muck and misery of WWI; some of the furnishings, hidden away during WWII, were the ones actually used in 1918.

From the Somme American Cemetery, take the D1044, D1 and D1032 94km southwest towards Compiègne, then follow signs 8km east along the N1031 and D546 to Clairière de l'Armistice.

in winter. The on-site welcome centre offers guided tours.

The Drive » Head 5km east-southeast on the D73 through tiny Beaumont-Hamel, across a pretty valley, past the 36th (Ulster) Division Memorial (site of a Northern Irish war monument and a homey tearoom) and on to the easy-to-spot arches of the Thiepval Memorial.

❼ Thiepval

On a lonely, windswept hilltop, the towering Thiepval Memorial (p93) to 'the Missing of the Somme' marks the site of a German stronghold that was stormed on 1 July 1916 with un-

imaginable casualties. Thiepval catches visitors off guard, both with its monumentality and its staggering simplicity: inscribed below the enormous arch, which is visible from miles around, are the names of over 72,000 British and South African soldiers whose remains were never recovered or identified. The **Museum at Thiepval**, run by Péronne's outstanding Historial de la Grande Guerre (p47), opened in 2016.

The Drive » A 44km ride on the D73 and the D929 brings you to Amiens.

❽ Amiens (p96)

Amiens' attractive, pedestrianised city centre offers a relaxing break from the battlefields. Climb the north tower of breathtaking, 13th-century Cathédrale Notre Dame (p97), a Unesco World Heritage Site, for stupendous views of town; a free, 45-minute **light show** bathes the cathedral's façade in vivid medieval colours nightly in summer.

Across the Somme River, gondola-like boats offer tours of Amiens' vast market gardens, the Hortillonnages (p98), which have supplied the city with vegetables and flowers since the Middle Ages.

Literature buffs will love the Maison de Jules Verne (p98), the turreted home where Jules Verne wrote some of his best-known works of brain-tingling science fiction.

The Drive » Take the D1029 19km east to Villers-Bretonneux.

❾ Villers-Bretonneux

During WWI, 46,000 of Australia's 313,000 volunteer soldiers met their deaths on the Western Front (14,000 others perished elsewhere). In the village of Villers-Bretonneux, the Musée Franco-Australien (p93) displays a collection of highly personal WWI

Amiens

Australiana, including letters and photographs that evoke life on the front. The names of 10,722 Australian soldiers whose remains were never found are engraved on the base of the 32m-high Australian National War Memorial (p95), 2km north of town.

The Drive » From the Australian National War Memorial, take the D23 briefly north, then meander east through pretty rolling country, roughly paralleling the Somme River, along the D71, D1 and D1017 into Péronne.

TRIP HIGHLIGHT
⑩ Péronne

Housed in a fortified medieval château, Péronne's award-winning museum, **Historial de la Grande Guerre** (Museum of the Great War; ☑03 22 83 14 18; www.historial.org; Château de Péronne, place André Audinot, Péronne; adult/child incl audioguide €9/4.50; ⊗9.30am-6pm Apr-Oct, to 5pm Thu-Tue Nov–mid-Dec & late Jan-Mar), provides a superb overview of WWI's historical and cultural context, telling the story of the war chronologically, with equal space given to the French, British and German perspectives. Visually engaging exhibits, including period films and bone-chilling engravings by Otto Dix, capture the aesthetic sensibilities, enthusiasm, naive patriotism and unimaginable violence of the time.

For excellent English-language brochures about the battlefields, visit Péronne's tourist office (p96), opposite the museum.

The Drive » The American cemetery is 24km east-northeast of Péronne via the D6, D406 and D57.

----

⑪ Somme American Cemetery

In late September 1918, just six weeks before the end of WWI, American units – flanked by their Commonwealth allies – launched an assault on the Germans' heavily fortified Hindenburg Line. Some of the fiercest fighting took place near the village of Bony, on the sloping site now occupied by the 1844 Latin crosses and Stars of David of the serene **Somme American Cemetery** (☑03 23 66 87 20; www.abmc.gov; rue de la Libération, Bony; ⊗9am-5pm); the names of 333 other men whose remains were never recovered are inscribed on the walls of the **Memorial Chapel**.

The Drive » From here, it's an easy drive back to Arras (68km via the A26), Lille (95km via the A26 and A1) or Amiens (81km via the A1).

Destinations

Normandy (p50)
From the Norman invasion of England in 1066 to the D-Day landings of 1944, Normandy has long played an outsized role in European history.

Lille, Flanders & the Somme (p80)
When it comes to culture, cuisine, beer, shopping and dramatic views of land and sea – not to mention good old-fashioned friendliness – these regions compete with the best France has to offer.

Falaise d'Aval (p59), Étretat
GASPAR JANOS/SHUTTERSTOCK ©

From the Norman invasion of England in 1066 to the D-Day landings of 1944, Normandy has long played an outsized role in European history. Historical sights, including the incomparable Bayeux Tapestry, combined with Camembert, apples, cider, cream-rich cuisine and the very freshest fish and seafood, provide ample reasons to visit this accessible and beautiful region of France.

Normandy

History

Vikings invaded present-day Normandy in the 9th century, and some of them soon established settlements and adopted Christianity. In 911 French king Charles the Simple, of the Carolingian dynasty, and Viking chief Hrölfr agreed that the area around Rouen should be handed over to these Norsemen – or Normans, as they came to be known.

Throughout the Hundred Years War (1337–1453), the Duchy of Normandy seesawed between French and English rule. England dominated the region for some 30 years until France gained permanent control in 1450. In the 16th century, Normandy, a Protestant stronghold, was the scene of considerable fighting between Catholics and Huguenots.

More recently, the liberation of Western Europe from Nazi occupation began in earnest on the beaches of Normandy on D-Day, 6 June 1944. Much of Normandy was badly damaged during the fighting; the city of Le Havre, for example, was heavily bombed during the Allied bombing raids known as Operation Astonia in September 1944, resulting in over 2000 civilian deaths in that town alone.

SEINE-MARITIME

The Seine-Maritime *département* (adminstrative division) stretches along the chalk-white cliffs of the Côte d'Albâtre (Alabaster Coast) from Le Tréport via Dieppe to Le Havre, France's second-busiest port (after Marseille). With its history firmly bound up with the sea, the region offers visitors an engaging mix of small seaside villages and dramatic clifftop walks.

When you fancy a break from the bracing sea air, head inland to the lively, ancient and good-looking metropolis of Rouen, a favourite haunt of Claude Monet and Simone de Beauvoir and one of the most intriguing and history-infused cities in France's northeast.

Rouen

POP 111,000

With its soaring Gothic cathedral, beautifully restored medieval quarter, imposing ancient churches, excellent museums and vibrant cultural life, Rouen is one of Normandy's most engaging and historically rich destinations.

The city has endured a turbulent history. It was devastated by fire and plague several times during the Middle Ages, and was occupied by the English during the Hundred Years War. The young French heroine Joan of Arc (Jeanne d'Arc) was tried for heresy and burned at the stake in the central square in 1431. And during WWII, Allied bombing raids laid waste to large parts of the city, especially south of the cathedral.

◉ Sights & Activities

Cathédrale Notre Dame   CATHEDRAL
(www.cathedrale-rouen.net; place de la Cathédrale; ⊙2-7pm Mon, 9am-7pm Tue-Sat, 8am-6pm Sun Apr-Oct, shorter hours Nov-Mar) Rouen's stunning Gothic cathedral, built between the late 12th and 16th centuries, was famously the subject of a series of canvases painted by Monet at various times of the day and year. The 75m-tall Tour de Beurre (Butter Tower) was financed by locals in return for being allowed to eat butter during Lent – or so the story goes. A free sound-and-light spectacular is projected on the façade every night from June (at 11pm) to late September (at 9.30pm).

★ Historial Jeanne d'Arc   MUSEUM
(☑02 35 52 48 00; www.historial-jeannedarc.fr; 7 rue St-Romain; adult/child €10.50/7.50; ⊙10am-6pm Tue-Sun) For an introduction to the great 15th-century heroine and the events that earned her fame – and shortly thereafter condemnation – don't miss this excellent site. It's less of a museum, and more of an immersive, theatre-like experience, where you walk through medieval corridors and watch (and hear via headphones, in seven languages) the dramatic retelling of Joan's visions, her victories, the trial that sealed her fate, and the mythologising that followed in the years after her death.

Église St-Maclou   CHURCH
(place Barthélémy; ⊙10am-noon & 2-5.30pm Sat & Sun) This supreme example of the Flamboyant Gothic–style church was built between 1437 and 1521, but much of the decoration dates from the Renaissance. The church was heavily damaged in WWII and later restored. Note the detailed wood panelling in the porch of the church; also observe how many of the statues on the exterior stonework of the church are missing their heads (victims of the French Wars of Religion). Half-timbered houses that incline at curious angles can be found on nearby side streets.

Musée des Beaux-Arts   GALLERY
(☑02 35 71 28 40; www.mbarouen.fr; esplanade Marcel Duchamp; ⊙10am-6pm Wed-Mon) FREE Housed in a very grand structure flung up in 1870, Rouen's simply outstanding finearts museum features canvases by Rubens, Modigliani, Pissarro, Renoir, Sisley (lots) and, of course, several works by Monet, as well as a fine collection of Flemish oils. There's also one jaw-dropping painting by Caravaggio as well as a very serene cafe. Drop your bag in the lockers provided and follow the route through the galleries, arranged chronologically.

Musée Le Secq des Tournelles   MUSEUM
(☑02 35 71 28 40; www.museelesecqdestour nelles.fr; 2 rue Jacques Villon; ⊙2-6pm Wed-Mon) FREE Home to one of the world's premier collections of wrought iron, this riveting (excuse the pun) museum is an astonishing sight, showcasing the extraordinary skills of pre-industrial iron- and locksmiths, in

Gros Horloge (p53), Rouen
CATARINA BELOVA/SHUTTERSTOCK ©

51

Rouen

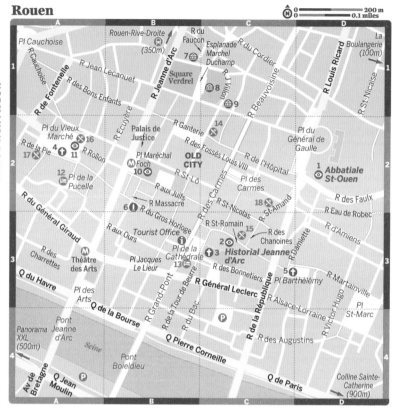

Rouen

a magnificent setting across two floors within a desanctified 16th-century church. There's everything from elaborate pen-knives to candle snuffs, beds, fortified chests, candelabra, miniature pistols and intricate keys.

Musée de la Céramique   MUSEUM
(☑02 35 07 31 74; www.museedelaceramique.fr; 1 rue du Faucon; ⊘2-6pm Wed-Mon) **FREE** The Ceramics Museum, housed in a 17th-century building with a fine courtyard, is known for its 16th- to 19th-century faience (tin-glazed earthenware) and porcelain. Don't miss

sculptural pieces such as the exquisite celestial sphere (1725) on the upper floor.

Église Jeanne d'Arc
CHURCH

(p39)

Gros Horloge
TOWER

(rue du Gros Horloge; adult/child €7/3.50; ⏰10am-1pm & 2-7pm Tue-Sun Apr-Oct, 2-6pm Nov-Mar) Spanning rue du Gros Horloge, the Great Clock's Renaissance archway has a gilded, one-handed medieval clock face on each side. High above, a Gothic belfry, reached via spiral stairs, affords spectacular views. The excellent audioguide is a great introduction to Rouen's colourful history and is available in eight languages.

Palais de Justice
ARCHITECTURE

(place Maréchal Foch & rue aux Juifs) The ornately Gothic Law Courts, little more than a shell at the end of WWII, have been restored to their early-16th-century glory. On rue Jeanne d'Arc, however, you can still see the very pock-marked façade, which shows the damage sustained during bombing raids in 1944. Around the corner on pedestrianised rue aux Juifs, you can peer into the spire- and gargoyle-adorned courtyard.

★ Abbatiale St-Ouen
CHURCH

(place du Général de Gaulle; ⏰10am-noon & 2-6pm Tue-Thu, Sat & Sun) This largely empty 14th-century abbey is a gloriously sublime and quite stunning example of the Rayonnant Gothic style, with a colossal interior dappled with the light from the gorgeous stained glass; it's quite a mind-blowing spectacle. The entrance is through the lovely garden on the south side, facing rue des Faulx.

Panorama XXL
GALLERY

(📱02 35 52 95 25; www.panoramxxl.com; quai de Boisguilbert; adult/child €9.50/6.50; ⏰10am-7pm Tue-Sun May-Aug, to 6pm Tue-Sun Sep-Apr) In a large, circular column on the waterfront, Panorama XXL is a massive 360-degree exhibition offering in-depth exploring of one astonishing landscape, created with photographs, drawings, digital images and recorded audio. Past years have featured the Great Barrier Reef, Amazonia, Ancient Rome and Rouen in 1431 – often with sunrise and sunset generating different moods, as well as storms. A 15m-high viewing platform in the middle of the room gives a fine vantage point over the scene.

A joint ticket with Historial Jeanne d'Arc is €15 for adults and €12 for children.

Colline Sainte-Catherine
HILL

(rue Henri Rivière) To size up Rouen, climb this hill rising up next to the Seine. It's a 15-minute walk to the summit, from where Monet once painted a view of the city. Sunrise or sunset casts the city in a fine photographic light, but wear good shoes as the climb can be slippery. As you walk along rue Henri Rivière, look out for the concrete steps to your right straight after the long brown building, which lead to wooden steps up the hill.

🛏 Sleeping

★ La Boulangerie
B&B €

(📱06 12 94 53 15; www.laboulangerie.fr; 59 rue St-Nicaise; s from €67, d €77-92; 🛜) Tucked away in a quiet side street 1.2km northeast of the cathedral, this adorable B&B sits above a historic bakery with three bright, pleasingly decorated rooms to its name, decorated with artwork and exposed beam ceilings. Charming host Aminata is a gold mine of local information. Parking available nearby for €5; breakfast is included.

Auberge de Jeunesse Robec
HOSTEL €

(📱02 35 08 18 50; www.fuaj.org; 3 rue du Tour; dm €25-35; ⏰reception 8-11.45am & 5.30-10pm; 🛜) The two- to eight-bed rooms at this modern, 88-bed hostel are comfortable and functional. It's set 2km east of the cathedral off rte de Darnétal; from the city centre, take bus T2 or T3 to the 'Auberge de Jeunesse' stop.

Les Cabanes du Clos Masure
COTTAGE €€

(📱07 70 36 84 21; www.cabanesclosmasure.fr; 873 rue du Bornier; r incl breakfast €140) Sleep in the rustling treetops in wood cabins located some 30 minutes northeast of Rouen at this fun place. It's also a working farm with cows and chickens running about, and a good choice for families with young children (cabins are small but cosy and

MEDIEVAL MEANDER

With its ghostly white-stone ruins glowing against bright green grass and dark green trees, the Abbaye de Jumièges (☑ 02 35 37 24 02; www.abbayedejumieges.fr; Jumièges; adult/child €6.50/free; ☺ 9.30am-6.30pm mid-Apr–mid-Sep, 9.30am-1pm & 2.30-5.30pm mid-Sep–mid-Apr) is one of Normandy's most evocative medieval relics. The church was begun in 1020, and William the Conqueror attended its consecration in 1067. The abbey declined during the Hundred Years War but enjoyed a renaissance under Charles VII, flourishing until revolutionaries booted out the monks in 1790 and allowed the buildings to be mined for construction material.

Jumièges is 28km from Rouen. To get there, take the westbound D982 and then, from Duclair, the D65.

sleep up to six). Breakfast is put in a basket, which you hoist up.

Hôtel Le Cardinal
HOTEL €€

(☑ 02 35 70 24 42; www.cardinal-hotel.fr; 1 place de la Cathédrale; s/d from €78/88; ☎) Facing the cathedral's famous west façade and with large portraits of namesake cardinals overlooking the small lobby, this 15-room hotel is one of the best midrange deals in central Rouen. All but two of the bright rooms have romantic cathedral views, and eight doubles come with balconies or terraces, including the suites. Buffet breakfast is €10.

Hôtel de Bourgtheroulde
LUXURY HOTEL €€€

(☑ 02 35 14 50 50; www.hotelsparouen.com; 15 place de la Pucelle; r €165-370; ﾟ✹☎✷) Rouen's finest hostelry (owned for the last five years by the Marriott) serves up a sumptuous mix of early-16th-century architecture – Flamboyant Gothic, to be precise – and sleek, modern luxury. The 78 rooms are spacious and gorgeously appointed. Amenities include a pool (18m), sauna and spa in the basement; the Atrium Bar has live piano music on Saturday evening.

✗ Eating

Hallettes du Vieux Marché
MARKET €

(place du Vieux Marché; ☺7am-7pm Tue-Sat, 7.30am-1pm Sun) This covered market by the Église Jeanne d'Arc has an excellent *from-agerie* (cheese shop) as well as fishmongers and other purveyors of foods.

Dame Cakes
PASTRIES €

(☑ 02 35 07 49 31; www.damecakes.fr; 70 rue St-Romain; lunch menus €16-20, tea & cake €9; ☺10.30am-7pm Mon-Sat; ✐) Walk through the grand and historic, early-20th-century façade and you'll discover a delightfully civilised selection of pastries, cakes and chocolates. From noon to 3pm you can tuck into delicious quiches, gratins and salads in the attached *salon de thé* (tearoom). Lovely.

Citizen
CAFE €

(4 rue de l'Écureuil; mains €7-13, Sat brunch €22; ☺9am-7pm Mon-Fri, from 11am Sat) Citizen is undeniably hip with its black lines, industrial fixtures and groovy tunes playing overhead. More important is the excellent coffee, and the tasty bites on hand (granola, fresh fruit and *fromage blanc* (white cheese) for breakfast; smoked salmon salad for lunch), plus beers from Brooklyn Brewery. The outdoor seating is popular when the sun is out.

★L'Espiguette
BISTRO €

(☑ 02 35 71 66 27; 25 place St-Amand; weekday lunch menus €13, mains €17-24; ☺noon-10pm Tue-Sat) This charmingly decorated eatery serves excellent bistro classics – think *osso bucco* (veal casserole), fillet of sole, beef tartare – with the day's offerings up on a chalkboard. It's quite popular with locals, so reserve ahead, even at lunchtime (the lunch *menu* is a great deal). Grab a seat at one of the outdoor tables on a warm day.

Bar à Huîtres
SEAFOOD €

(place du Vieux Marché; mains €10-16, oysters per half-dozen/dozen from €10/17; ☺10am-2pm Tue-Sat) Grab a seat at the horseshoe-shaped bar at this casual but polished eatery located inside Rouen's covered market for uberfresh seafood. Specials change daily based on what's fresh, from giant shrimp to dorado and fillet of sole, but each is cooked to perfection. Don't neglect the restaurant's namesake – the satisfying *huîtres* (oysters) with several different varieties on offer.

Les Nymphéas
GASTRONOMY €€€

(☑ 09 74 56 46 19; www.lesnympheas-rouen.fr; 7 rue de la Pie; weekday lunch menus €27, other menus €40-77, mains €33-58; ☺12.15-2pm Tue-Sun, 7-9pm Tue-Sat) With its formal tables arrayed under 16th-century beams, Les Nymphéas has long been a top address for fine dining in Rouen. Young chef Alexandre

Dessaux serves up French cuisine that manages to be both traditional and creative. Reservations are a must on weekends. A vegan menu is available for either €30 or €39.

ℹ Information

Tourist Office (☏ 02 32 08 32 40; www. rouentourisme.com; 25 place de la Cathédrale; ☺ 9am-7pm Mon-Sat, 9.30am-12.30pm & 2-6pm Sun May-Sep, 9.30am-12.30pm & 1.30-6pm Mon-Sat Oct-Apr)

ℹ Getting Around

BICYCLE

Cy'clic (☏ 08 00 08 78 00; http://cyclic.rouen. fr; ☺ 5am-1am), lets you rent a city bike from 24 locations. Credit-card registration for one/ seven days costs €1/7, plus a deposit of €150. Use is free for the first 30 minutes; the second/ third/fourth and subsequent half-hours cost €1/2/4 each.

BUS & METRO

Rouen's public transport is operated by Réseau Astuce (www.crea-astuce.fr). A single-journey ticket costs €1.60.

CAR

Free parking is available near the Boulingrin metro terminus, 1.5km northeast of the cathedral (arrive before 7am or after 7pm for better luck getting a spot), and at Parking du Mont Riboudet (next to the Palais des Sports), 2.7km northeast of the cathedral; the latter is linked to the centre by buses T1, T2 and T3.

Dieppe

POP 30,600

A seaside resort since 1824, Dieppe hasn't been chic for over a century, but the town's lack of cuteness and pretension can be refreshing. During WWII, the city was the focal point of the only large-scale Allied raid on Nazi-occupied France before D-Day, a catastrophic event commemorated in one of the town's top museums.

Dieppe was one of France's most important ports in the 16th and 17th centuries, when ships regularly sailed from here to West Africa and Brazil. Many of the earliest French settlers in Canada set sail from Dieppe.

⊙ Sights & Activities

Château-Musée MUSEUM
(☏ 02 35 06 61 99; www.dieppe.fr; rue de Chastes; adult/child €4.50/free; ☺ 10am-noon & 2-5pm Wed-Sun Oct-May, 10am-6pm Wed-Sun Jun-Sep) Built between the 14th and 18th centuries, this imposing clifftop castle affords spectacular views of the coast. Inside, the museum explores the city's maritime history as well as displaying a remarkable collection of carved ivory. There are also local scenes painted by artists such as Pissarro and Renoir between 1870 and 1915, when Dieppe was at the height of its popularity with the fashionable, holidaying classes.

Abbaye de Jumiéges

THE DIEPPE RAID

On 19 August 1942 a mainly Canadian force of over 6000, backed up by 300 ships and 800 aircraft, landed on 20km of beaches between Berneval-sur-Mer and Varengeville-sur-Mer. The objectives: to help the Soviets by drawing Nazi military power away from the Eastern Front and – so the film *Dieppe Uncovered* revealed in 2012 – to 'pinch' one of the Germans' new, four-rotor Enigma encoding machines (the effort failed). The results of the Dieppe Raid were nothing short of catastrophic: 73% of the men who took part ended up killed, wounded or missing-in-action. But lessons learnt at great cost here proved invaluable in planning the Normandy landings two years later.

For insights into the operation, visit Dieppe's **Memorial du 19 Août 1942** (www.dieppe-operationjubilee-19aout1942.fr; place Camille St-Saëns; adult/child €3.50/free; ⊕2-6.30pm Wed-Mon late May-Sep, to 6pm Thu, Fri, Sat, Sun & holidays late Mar–mid-May, Fri, Sat & Sun Oct–mid-Nov, closed mid-Nov–Mar).

Cité de la Mer   MUSEUM

(Estran; ☑02 35 06 93 20; www.estrancitedelamer.fr; 37 rue de l'Asile Thomas; adult/child €7.50/4; ⊕9.30am-6pm Mon-Fri, 9.30am-12.30pm & 1.30-6pm Sat & Sun) The 'City of the Sea' brings Dieppe's long maritime and fishing history to life, with kid-friendly exhibits that include model ships and a fish-petting *bassin tactile*. Sea creatures native to the English Channel swim in a dozen aquariums. Ask for an English-language brochure at the ticket desk.

Dieppe Canadian War Cemetery   CEMETERY

(Cimetière Canadien; www.cwgc.org) Many of the Canadians who died in the Dieppe Raid of 1942 are buried at this peaceful site framed by rolling fields. The cemetery is situated 4km towards Rouen; from the centre, take av des Canadiens (the continuation of av Gambetta) south and follow the signs.

Beach   BEACH

(🔊) Dieppe's often-windy beach is a 1.8km-long stretch of smooth pebbles, rather like the beach at Brighton across the channel. The vast lawns were laid out in the 1860s by that seashore-loving imperial duo, Napoléon III and his wife, Eugénie. The area has several play areas for kids.

☞ Tours

Ville de Dieppe   BOATING

(☑06 09 52 37 38; www.bateau-ville-de-dieppe.com; quai Henri IV; adult €9-18, child €5.50-14; ⊕weekends & school holidays Apr-Nov & mid-Jul-mid-Aug) Hop aboard one of these boat excursions (35 to 90 minutes) along the dramatic cliffs of the Côte d'Albâtre to get the coastline in perspective. The company also offers sea fishing.

🛏 Sleeping

Villa Les Capucins   B&B €

(☑02 35 82 16 52; www.villadescapucins.jimdo.com; 11 rue des Capucins; d/tr €80/100) Run by a retired lady, this B&B is a good surprise, not least for the marvellous sense of peacefulness that envelops the property (it's a former convent) – all just a two-minute walk east of the harbour. The four rooms are nicely appointed with antique furniture, framed artwork and homey touches, and the ravishing landscaped garden is perfect for unwinding.

Les Arcades   HOTEL €

(☑02 35 84 14 12; www.lesarcades.fr; 1-3 arcades de la Bourse; d €75-92; ☎) Perched above a colonnaded arcade from the 1600s, this well-managed and long-established place enjoys a great location by the port. The decor, in tans and browns, is unexciting, but 12 of the 21 rooms have fine port views (the cheaper ones face the road). Breakfast is €10.

Hôtel de la Plage   HOTEL €€

(☑02 35 84 18 28; www.plagehotel-dieppe.com; 20 bd de Verdun; d €77-119, f €95-130; Ｐ☎) One of several somewhat faded seafront places, this hotel has 40 modern, mod-con rooms of varying shapes and sizes, including family rooms; those at the front have balconies and afford knockout views of the sea. Cheaper rooms face into the courtyard. Parking €8.

✖ Eating

Dieppe has a decent range of quality seafood restaurants. Quai Henri IV, along the north side of the harbour, is lined with touristy choices.

Le Turbot
FRENCH €€

(☑ 02 35 82 63 44; 12 quai Cale; mains €18-27, menus €16; ⊗12.15-2.30pm & 7.15-9.30pm Tue-Sat) A prime place for lunch or dinner, this family-run Norman bistro decked out in sea paraphernalia serves outstanding seafood. Fresh-off-the-boat dishes, such as monkfish, Dover sole, scallops, and ray in cream sauce and capers, vie with deftly prepared meat dishes. At €17, the prix-fixe *menu* (which also includes a buffet selection of seafood entrées) is good value.

À La Marmite Dieppoise
SEAFOOD €€

(☑ 02 35 84 24 26; 8 rue St-Jean; menus €21-44, mains €16-36; ⊗noon-2pm Tue-Sun, plus 7-9pm Tue-Sat) This Dieppe institution is applauded for its hearty and rich *marmite dieppoise* (cream-sauce stew made with mussels, prawns and four kinds of fish – though you can also order it with lobster), served in a rustic dining room: it's a dish to remember. Other specialities include Normandy-style fish and, from October to May, scallops.

Les Voiles d'Or
GASTRONOMY €€€

(☑ 02 35 84 16 84; www.lesvoilesdor.fr; 2 chemin des Falaise; mains €35-38, lunch menus €39, dinner menus €56; ⊗noon-1 & 8-9pm Wed-Sat, noon-1pm Sun) For cutting-edge cuisine concocted from top-quality ingredients, this Michelin-starred place is worth seeking out. Chef Christian Arhan has a soft spot for local seafood but the menu also includes savoury meat dishes. Just next door is Villa Bali-Dieppe (same owners), an excellent B&B featuring three rooms decorated in a Balinese style (doubles €130). It's near Église Notre-Dame de Bon Secours.

ⓘ Information

Tourist Office (☑ 02 32 14 40 60; www.dieppe tourisme.com; Pont Jehan Ango; ⊗9am-1pm & 2-5pm Mon-Sat year-round, plus 9.30am-1pm & 2-5.30pm Sun May-Sep)

Côte d'Albâtre

Stretching along the Norman coast for 130km, the vertical, bone-white cliffs of the Côte d'Albâtre (Alabaster Coast) are strikingly reminiscent of the limestone cliffs of Dover, right across the Channel. The dramatic coastline, sculpted over aeons by wind and waves, is dotted with attractive villages, fishing harbours, resort towns, pebbly beaches, eroded rock forms and gorgeous gardens.

St-Valery-en-Caux
POP 4200

This delightful coastal village, 32km west of Dieppe, has a large fishing and pleasure port, a lovely beach and half a dozen hotels. It is also the site of a Franco-British WWII cemetery. In January 1945, a runaway troop train crashed here, killing 89 American soldiers.

🛏 Sleeping & Eating

La Maison des Galets
HOTEL €

(☑ 02 35 97 11 22; www.lamaisondesgalets.fr; 6 rue des Remparts, St-Valery-en-Caux; s €50, d €70-80; 🛇) The spacious lobby is classic 1950s, with leather couches and lovely sea panoramas. Upstairs, the 14 rooms are pretty and simply furnished, with nautical touches and shiny all-tile bathrooms, with pricier rooms getting views of the waters. La Maison des Galets is situated 100m west of the casino.

Restaurant du Port
SEAFOOD €€

(☑ 02 35 97 08 93; 18 quai d'Amont, St-Valery-en-Caux; menus €27-49, mains €13-38; ⊗12.15-2 & 7.30-9pm Tue, Wed, Fri & Sat, noon-1pm Sun) A treat for lovers of fish and seafood (*fruits de mer*), this restaurant down by the port has been doing good business since 1989. À la carte offerings include oysters, fresh crab and turbot marinated in hollandaise sauce. The seafood platters (€43) are a sight to behold.

DON'T MISS

VEULES-LES-ROSES

With its wonderfully relaxing atmosphere and lovely setting, Veules-les-Roses is one of the Côte d'Albâtre's gems. The pebbly beach is never too crowded and the flowery village is supremely picturesque, with elegant mansions and an imposing church. The small river running through the village adds to the bucolic appeal – it also makes it into the record books as France's shortest river flowing into the sea. Look out for the *cressonnières* (ponds where watercress is grown). You can find Veules-les-Roses 8km east of St-Valery-en-Caux.

Cliffs, Fécamp
CHRISTIAN MUSAT/SHUTTERSTOCK ©

Fécamp

POP 19.300

Fécamp is a lively fishing port with an attractive harbour, dramatic cliffs and a long monastic history. It is best known for producing Bénédictine, a fiery 'medicinal elixir' concocted here by a Venetian monk in 1510. Lost during the Revolution, the recipe was rediscovered in the 19th century. The Abbatiale de la Ste-Trinité was a sacred place of pilgrimage during the Middle Ages for drops of Jesus' blood enshrined there.

◎ Sights & Activities

Abbatiale de la Ste-Trinité   ABBEY
(place des Ducs Richard; ⊙9am-7pm Apr-Sep, 9am-noon & 2-5pm Oct-Mar) Built from 1175 to 1220 by Richard the Lionheart, towering Abbatiale de la Ste-Trinité was the most important pilgrimage site in Normandy until the construction of Mont St-Michel, thanks to the drops of Jesus' blood that, legend has it, miraculously floated to Fécamp in the trunk of a fig tree, landing on a beach nearby. Across from the abbey are the remains of a fortified **château** built in the 10th and 11th centuries by the earliest dukes of Normandy.

Palais de la Bénédictine   LIQUEUR FACTORY
(p27)

Les Pêcheries   MUSEUM
(Musée de Fécamp; ☑02 35 28 31 99; 3 quai Capitaine Jean Recher; adult/child €7/free; ⊙11am-

7pm May-Sep, 11am-5.30pm Wed-Mon Oct-Apr) Fécamp's new flagship museum is a terrific addition to town, situated in the middle of the harbour, 300m northwest of the tourist office and showcasing local history, the town's fishing industry, local artists and traditional Norman life. The dramatic, glassed-in observation platform on top offers great views across Fécamp. The audioguide is €2.

Plage de Fécamp   BEACH
This smooth-pebble beach stretches southward from the narrow channel connecting the port with the open sea. In summer it's loads of fun, and you can rent catamarans, kayaks, paddle boats and windsurfers.

Cap Fagnet   VIEWPOINT
The highest point on the Côte d'Albâtre, Cap Fagnet (110m) towers over Fécamp from the north, offering fantastic views up and down the coast. The site of an important German *blockhaus* and radar station during WWII, today it's topped by a chapel and there are five wind turbines a short walk to the east (there's a plan to erect 83 more turbines offshore, due to generate power from 2021). Cap Fagnet is a 1.5km walk from the centre.

🛏 Sleeping

Camping de Renéville   CAMPGROUND €
(☑02 35 28 20 97; www.campingdereneville.com; chemin de Nesmond; tent & 2 adults from €14; ⊙Apr-Oct) Dramatically situated on the western cliffs overlooking the beach, this campground also rents out two- and six-person chalets (from €280 per week). In July and August the tent rate goes up to €17.

Hôtel Vent d'Ouest   HOTEL €
(☑02 35 28 04 04; www.hotelventdouest.tm.fr; 3 rue Gambetta; d €57-65, q €95) Small and welcoming, with a smart breakfast room and 15 pleasant rooms decorated in yellow and blue. Call ahead if you'll be checking in after 8pm. The hotel is situated 200m east (up the hill) from the port, next to Église St-Étienne. Buffet breakfast is €8.

Le Grand Pavois   HOTEL €€
(☑02 35 10 01 01; www.hotel-grand-pavois.com; 15 quai de la Vicomté; r/ste from €103/149; [P] 🛜) This reliable three-star hotel has a fine location overlooking the marina, and it's an easy stroll to the beach. The welcome is warm, and the spacious rooms have attractive furnishings and comfortable mattresses, though the big windows – and the view! – are undoubtedly the best features.

Eating

Tourist-oriented crêperies and restaurants, many specialising in fish and mussels, line the south side of the port, along quai de la Vicomté and nearby parts of quai Bérigny.

Le Daniel's FRENCH €€
(☑ 02 76 39 95 68; 5 place Nicolas Selle; lunch menus €15-17, dinner menus €24-40; ⊙ noon-2pm & 7-9pm Tue-Sat) Tucked down a narrow lane just a short stroll from the marina, this delightful spot serves up market-fresh fare that highlights delicacies from the region including Valmont trout, creamy rich oysters and braised veal. The service is warm, and the plates are beautifully presented – great value. Just be sure to call ahead for a table as it's not big.

La Marée SEAFOOD €€
(☑ 02 35 29 39 15; www.restaurant-maree-fecamp. fr; 77 quai Bérigny; mains €17-27, menus €19-29.50; ⊙ noon-2pm & 7.30-8.30pm Tue, Wed, Fri & Sat, noon-2pm Thu & Sun; 🖬) Locals claim that you won't find better seafood anywhere in town than here: fish and seafood – that's all that matters at quayside La Marée, Fécamp's premier address for maritime dining, with outside terrace.

ⓘ Information

Tourist Office (☑ 02 35 28 51 01; www.fecamp tourisme.com; quai Sadi Carnot; ⊙ 9am-6pm Mon-Fri, from 10am Sat & Sun; 🤶) Has useful English-language brochures and maps and free luggage lockers. Situated at the eastern end of the pleasure port, across the parking lot from the train station.

ⓘ Getting Around

The tourist office rents bicycles for €9/14/40 per day/weekend/week.

Étretat

POP 1500

The small and delightful village of Étretat's dramatic coastal scenery – it's framed by twin cliffs – made it a favourite of painters such as Camille Corot, Eugène Boudin, Gustave Courbet and Claude Monet. With the vogue for sea air at the end of the 19th century, fashionable Parisians came and built extravagant villas.

Étretat has never gone out of style and still swells with visitors every weekend, who sit on the shingle beach, wander up and

down the shoreline or clamber up to the fantastic vantage points above the chalk cliffs.

◉ Sights & Activities

The pebbly beach is separated from the town centre by a dyke. To the left as you face the sea, you can see the Falaise d'Aval, renowned for its beautiful arch – and the adjacent Aiguille, a needle of rock poking high up from the waves.

To the right as you face the sea towers the Falaise d'Amont, atop of which a memorial marks the spot where two aviators were last seen before attempting to cross the Atlantic in 1927.

The tourist office has a map of trails around town and can also provide details on sail-powered cruises aboard a two-masted schooner (⊙ Mar-Oct).

🛏 Sleeping

★ **Detective Hôtel** HOTEL €
(☑ 02 35 27 01 34; www.detectivehotel.com; 6 av Georges V; d €59-129; 🤶) Run by a former detective with an impressive moustache, this establishment was inspired by Sherlock Holmes and Hercule Poirot. Each of the 14 charming rooms bears the name of a fictional gumshoe whose time and place have inspired the decor. In some, the first mystery you'll face is how to find the secret door to the hidden bathroom. Utterly original.

ⓘ Information

Tourist Office (☑ 02 35 27 05 21; www.etretat. net; place Maurice Guillard; ⊙ 9.30am-6.30pm mid-Jun–mid-Sep, 10am-noon & 2-6pm Mon-Sat mid-Sep–mid-Jun, Sun during school holidays)

Le Havre

POP 176,000

A Unesco World Heritage Site since 2005 and a regular port of call for cruise ships, Le Havre is a love letter to modernism, evoking, more than any other French city, France's postwar energy and optimism. All but obliterated in September 1944 by Allied bombing raids that killed 3000 civilians, the centre was completely rebuilt by the Belgian architect Auguste Perret – mentor to Le Corbusier – whose bright, airy modernist vision remains, miraculously, largely intact.

Attractions include a museum full of captivating impressionist paintings, a soaring modernist church with a mesmerising

NATURE WATCH

Inland from Utah Beach, to the south and southwest, is the 1480-sq-km **Parc Naturel Régional des Marais du Cotentin et du Bessin** (www. parc-cotentin-bessin.fr), a vast expanse of waterways, marshes, moors and hedgerows. The Maison du Parc (visitor centre) is in St-Côme-du-Mont, 50km west of Bayeux just off the N13.

For details on hiking and cycling in the park and elsewhere in the Manche *département*, visit www.manche-tourism.com and click on 'Walks, Rambles & Rides' under the 'Explore' tab.

stained-glass tower, hilltop gardens with views over the city and a medieval church that rose again from the ashes of war.

⊙ Sights

Musée Malraux   MUSEUM
(p30)

Église St-Joseph   CHURCH
(bd François 1er; ⊙10am-6pm) Perret's masterful, 107m-high Église St-Joseph, visible from all over town, was built using bare concrete from 1951 to 1959. Some 13,000 panels of coloured glass make the soaring, sombre interior particularly striking when it's sunny. Stained-glass artist Marguerite Huré created a cohesive masterpiece in her collaboration with Perret, and her use of shading and colour was thoughtfully conceived, evoking different moods depending on where the sun is in the sky – and the ensuing colours created by the illumination.

Jardins Suspendus   GARDENS
(rue du Fort; gardens free, greenhouses €2; ⊙10.30am-8pm Apr-Sep, to 5pm Oct-Mar) The Jardins Suspendus (Hanging Garden) is an old hilltop fortress transformed into a beautiful set of gardens, whose greenhouses and outdoor spaces feature exquisite flowers, trees and grasses from five different continents, as fine views range over the harbour. It's a 30-minute uphill walk from the centre, or you can catch bus 1 along bd François 1er near the beach.

Le Volcan   CULTURAL CENTRE
(Espace Oscar Niemeyer; ☑02 35 19 10 10; www.levolcan.com; place du Général de Gaulle; ⊙library

10am-7pm) Le Havre's most conspicuous landmark, designed by Brazilian architect Oscar Niemeyer and opened in 1982, is also the city's premier cultural venue. One look and you'll understand how it got its name, which means 'the volcano' – it's quite a sight, especially framed against a blue sky. Extensive renovations saw the complex reopen with a new concert hall and an ultramodern *mediathèque* (multimedia library). It's situated at the western end of the Bassin du Commerce, the city centre's former port.

Appartement Témoin   ARCHITECTURE
(☑02 35 22 31 22; 181 rue de Paris; adult/child €5/free; ⊙tours 3.30pm & 4.30pm Wed & Fri, 2.30pm, 3.30pm & 4.30pm Sat, 10.30am, 11.30am, 2.30pm, 3.30pm & 4.30pm Sun) Furnished in impeccable early-1950s style, this lovingly furnished bourgeois apartment can be visited on a one-hour guided tour that starts at 181 rue de Paris (Maison du Patrimoine). The apartment is a remarkable time capsule of the postwar boom days that Le Havre experienced, complete with clothes, newspapers, furniture and appliances exactly as one would have seen entering a downtown apartment in the decade of the city's reconstruction. Reservations are recommended as there are 19 places per visit.

Cathédrale Notre-Dame   CHURCH
When Le Havre's concrete expanses and straight lines overpower you, stop by this lovely Baroque church, which somehow eluded the intense bombing efforts of the Royal Air Force. The cathedral originally dates to the early 16th century and is the oldest building in the centre of town; the interior is a repository of calm.

🛏 Sleeping

Hôtel le Petit Vatel   HOTEL €
(☑02 35 41 72 07; www.lepetitvatel.com; 86 rue Louis Brindeau; s/d €60/70; @ 🖨) This central spot earns high marks for comfortable rooms, a good location and very kind staff. Rooms receive decent natural light, the mattresses are fresh, and the tiled bathrooms are spick and span. There's a small, sunny lounge on the ground floor. Breakfast is €9.

Hôtel Oscar   HOTEL €
(☑02 35 42 39 77; www.hotel-oscar.fr; 106 rue Voltaire; s €49-79, d €50-109; 🖨) A treat for architecture aficionados, this bright and very central hotel brings Auguste Perret's mid-20th-century legacy alive. The rooms

are authentic retro, with hardwood floors and large windows, as is the tiny 1950s lounge. Reception closes at 8.30pm. It's situated across the street from Le Volcan, with some rooms looking straight onto it. Breakfast is €9.

★Hôtel Vent d'Ouest BOUTIQUE HOTEL €€

(☑ 02 35 42 50 69; www.ventdouest.fr; 4 rue de Caligny; d €100-150, ste €170, apt €185; ☎) This terrific and very stylish four-star establishment is all nautical downstairs and has cheerfully painted rooms upstairs arranged with sisal flooring and attractive furnishings; ask for one with a balcony. There are lovely common areas where you can while away the hours with a book when the weather inevitably sours, including an enticing cafe-bar with leather armchairs.

✖ Eating

Halles Centrales MARKET €

(rue Voltaire; ☺8.30am-7.30pm Mon-Sat, 9am-1pm Sun) The food stalls at Le Havre's main market include a patisserie, a *fromagerie* and many tempting fruit stands; there's also a small supermarket here. You can find it a block west of Le Volcan.

★La Taverne Paillette BRASSERIE €€

(☑ 02 35 41 31 50; www.taverne-paillette.com; 22 rue Georges Braque; lunch menus €16-32, mains €16-26; ☺noon-midnight daily) Solid brasserie food is served up at this Le Havre institution

whose origins, in a former incarnation, go back to the late 16th century. Think bowls overflowing with mussels, generous salads, gargantuan seafood platters and, in the Alsatian tradition, eight types of *choucroute* (sauerkraut). Diners leave contentedly well-fed and many are here for its famous beer too.

Les Pieds Dans L'Eau SEAFOOD €€

(☑ 02 35 47 97 45; promenade de la Plage; mains €13-20; ☺noon-10pm) Amid the many simple restaurants set on the beach promenade, this place always draws a crowd for its reasonably priced seafood plates and ample prix-fixe *menus*. The mussels (served seven different ways) are a highlight, as are the oysters and grilled *dorade* (gilt-head bream).

La Petite Auberge FRENCH €€€

(☑ 02 35 46 27 32; www.lapetiteauberge-lehavre.fr; 32 rue de Ste-Adresse; mains €27-45, menus €25-43; ☺noon-9.30pm Tue & Thu-Sat, 7.30-9.30pm Wed, noon-4pm Sun) This absolute gem of a place has a low-beamed dining room that whispers of romance, while the dishes rarely fail to satisfy. The à la carte menu is limited (typically just two seafood and two meat dishes), but serves as a showcase for seasonal ingredients. There's a kids menu for €11.

❶ Information

Maison du Patrimoine (☑ 02 35 22 31 22; 181 rue de Paris; ☺2-6pm Mon-Sat, 10am-1pm

Église St-Joseph, Le Havre

& 2-6pm Sun) The tourist office's city centre annexe has an exhibition on Perret's postwar reconstruction of the city.

Tourist Office (☑ 02 32 74 04 04; www. lehavretourisme.com; 186 bd Clemenceau; ☺2-6pm Mon, 10am-12.30pm & 2-6pm Tue-Sat Nov-Mar, 9.30am-1pm & 2-7pm Apr-Nov) Has a map in English for a two-hour walking tour of Le Havre's architectural highlights and details on cultural events. Situated at the western edge of the city centre, one block south of the La Plage tram terminus.

CALVADOS

The Calvados *département* (www.calvados-tourisme.com) stretches from Honfleur in the east to Isigny-sur-Mer in the west and includes Caen, Bayeux and the D-Day beaches. The area is famed for its rich pastures and farm products, including butter, cheese, cider and an eponymous apple brandy.

The origins of the name 'Calvados' are opaque. One (tenuous) theory points to a (possibly mythical) ship of the Spanish Armada sent by King Philip II of Spain to attack England called *San El Salvador,* which was shipwrecked off the Normandy coast. Another more convincing argument attests the name derives from a pair of rocks off the Normandy coast known as *calva dorsa.*

Bayeux

POP 13,900

Two cross-Channel invasions, almost 900 years apart, gave Bayeux a front-row seat at defining moments in Western history. The dramatic story of the Norman invasion of England in 1066 is told in 58 vivid scenes by the world-famous and quite astonishing Bayeux Tapestry, embroidered just a few years after William the Bastard, Duke of Normandy, became William the Conqueror, King of England.

On 6 June 1944, 160,000 Allied troops, supported by almost 7000 naval vessels, stormed ashore along the coast just north of town. Bayeux was the first French town to be liberated (on the morning of 7 June 1944) and is one of the few places in Calvados to have survived WWII practically unscathed.

A very attractive and historic town, Bayeux makes an ideal base for exploring the D-Day beaches and is crammed with 13th- to 18th-century buildings plus a fine Gothic cathedral.

⊙ Sights

A 'triple ticket' good for all three of Bayeux' outstanding municipal museums (adult/child two museums €12/10, three museums €15/13.50) is available.

★**Bayeux Tapestry**   MUSEUM
(☑02 31 51 25 50; www.bayeuxmuseum.com; 15bis rue de Nesmond; adult/child incl audioguide €9.50/5; ☺9.30am-12.30pm & 2-5.30pm Mon-Sat, 10am-1pm & 2-5.30pm Sun Feb, Mar, Nov & Dec, to 6pm Apr-Jun, Sep & Oct, 9am-7pm Mon-Sat, 9am-1pm & 2-6pm Sun Jul & Aug, closed Jan) The world's most celebrated embroidery depicts the conquest of England by William the Conqueror in 1066 from an unashamedly Norman perspective. Commissioned by Bishop Odo of Bayeux, William's half-brother, for the opening of Bayeux's cathedral in 1077, the well-preserved cartoon strip tells the dramatic, bloody tale with verve and vividness as well as some astonishing artistry. Particularly incredible is its length – nearly 70m long – and the fine attention to detail.

Fifty-eight action-packed scenes of pageantry and mayhem occupy the centre of the canvas, while religious allegories and illustrations of everyday 11th-century life, some of them bawdy and naughty, adorn the borders. The final showdown at the Battle of Hastings is depicted in graphic fashion, complete with severed limbs and decapitated heads (along the bottom of scene 52). Halley's Comet, which blazed across the sky in 1066, appears in scene 32.

A 16-minute film gives the conquest historical, political and cultural context, including crucial details on the grooming habits of Norman and Saxon knights. Also well worth a listen is the lucid and highly informative panel-by-panel audioguide, available in 14 languages. A special audioguide for kids aged seven to 12 is available in French and English.

★**Musée d'Art et d'Histoire Baron Gérard**   MUSEUM
(MAHB; ☑02 31 92 14 21; www.bayeuxmuseum. com; 37 rue du Bienvenu; adult/child €7.50/5; ☺9.30am-6.30pm May-Sep, 10am-12.30pm & 2-6pm Oct-Apr, closed 3 weeks in Jan) Make sure you drop by this museum – one of France's most gorgeously presented provincial museums – where exhibitions cover everything from Gallo-Roman archaeology through medieval art to paintings from the Renaissance and on to the 20th century,

Bayeux

Bayeux

including a fine work by Gustave Caillebotte. Other highlights include impossibly fine local lace and Bayeux-made porcelain. The museum is housed in the former bishop's palace.

A joint ticket for admission to the Musée d'Art et d'Histoire Baron Gérard and either the Bayeux Tapestry or the Musée Mémorial de la Bataille de Normandie is €12 (or €15 for all three).

LEONID ANDRONOV/SHUTTERSTOCK ©

Pont de Normandie

Cathédrale Notre Dame CATHEDRAL
(rue du Bienvenu; ⊙ 8.30am-7pm) Most of Bayeux's spectacular Norman Gothic cathedral dates from the 13th century, though the crypt (take the stairs on the north side of the choir), the arches of the nave and the lower parts of the entrance towers are 11th-century Romanesque. The central tower was added in the 15th century; the copper dome dates from the 1860s. The crypt, with its colourful frescoes, is a highlight. Several plaques and stained-glass windows commemorate American and British sacrifices during the world wars.

Musée Mémorial de la Bataille de Normandie MUSEUM
(p22)

Bayeux War Cemetery CEMETERY
(p22)

Conservatoire de la Dentelle MUSEUM
(Lace Conservatory; ☑ 02 31 92 73 80; http://dentelledebayeux.free.fr; 6 rue du Bienvenu; ⊙ 9.30am-12.30pm & 2.30-6pm Mon-Sat, to 5pm Mon & Thu) **FREE** Lacemaking (*dentellerie*), brought to Bayeux by nuns in 1678, once employed 5000 people. The industry is sadly long gone, but at the Conservatoire you can watch some of France's most celebrated lacemakers create intricate designs using dozens of bobbins and hundreds of pins; a small shop also sells some of their delicate creations. The half-timbered building housing the work-

shop, decorated with carved wooden figures, dates from the 1400s.

🛏 Sleeping

Camping des Bords de L'Aure CAMPGROUND €
(☑ 02 31 92 08 43; www.camping-bayeux.fr; bd d'Eindhoven; campsite from €13) This three-star municipal campground in the north of Bayeux has 140 sites pleasantly located near the River Aure. There's free access for campers to the municipal swimming pool, a short walk to the south. You can also rent out mobile homes (from €75 per night). Click on the website for a map of the campground.

Hôtel Reine Mathilde HOTEL €
(☑ 0231920813; www.hotel-bayeux-reinemathilde. fr; 23 rue Larcher; d/ste from €50/90, studio from €95; ☎) Occupying a superbly central location, this friendly hotel has comfortable accommodation, with an assortment of sleek and spacious rooms in the annexe, a converted barn by the Aure River. Rooms, named after historic figures, are attractively designed with beamed ceilings, and elegant lines, excellent lighting and modern bathrooms; studios come with a small kitchenette. A decent restaurant is also on-site.

Hotel Churchill HOTEL €€
(☑ 02 31 21 31 80; www.hotel-churchill.fr; 14-16 rue St-Jean; d €125-157, ste €179; ☎) Run by the affable ex–French first division foot-

baller Eric Pean, this terrific 46-room old town place by the cathedral has very decent accommodation with new carpets and 14 spotless modern rooms in the new extension. The hotel arranges daily morning shuttle bus trips to Mont St-Michel (€65, including admission).

Hôtel d'Argouges HOTEL €€
(☑ 02 31 92 88 86; www.hotel-dargouges.com; 21 rue St-Patrice; s/d €120/141, ste €210-295; ⊙ closed Dec & Jan; P 🛜) Occupying a very stately 18th-century residence with a lush little garden, this graceful and serene hotel has 28 comfortable rooms with exposed beams, thick walls and Louis XVI–style furniture, plus very welcoming and professional service, with excellent English spoken. The breakfast room, hardly changed since 1734, still has its original wood panels and parquet floors.

Villa Lara BOUTIQUE HOTEL €€€
(☑ 02 31 92 00 55; www.hotel-villalara.com; 6 place du Québec; d €200-420, ste €380-570; P ✳ 🛜) This modern and very elegant 28-room hotel concocts an appealing blend of minimalist colour schemes, top-quality fabrics and decor juxtaposing 18th- and 21st-century tastes. Amenities include a bar, a gym and a comfortable library-lounge with a fireplace. Most rooms have cathedral views and are well-equipped and decorated most tastefully, with attractive bathrooms.

Château de la Ferrière HISTORIC HOTEL €€€
(☑ 02 31 21 13 39; www.chateaudelaferriere.com; Vaux-sur-Aure; d incl breakfast from €220; P 🛜) Located between Bayeux and Longues-sur-Mer, this splendid 18th-century château – set in 13.4 hectares of lawn and woodland – is a handsome and elegant base for exploring the D-Day beaches and nearby sights. The huge rooms are littered with antique furniture and long curtains that reach either wooden or parquet floors, with lovely views extending over the gardens.

✕ Eating

★ La Reine Mathilde PASTRIES €
(☑ 02 31 92 00 59; 47 rue St-Martin; cakes from €2.50; ⊙ 9am-7.30pm Tue-Sun) With a vast expanse of glass in its windows and set with white-painted cast-iron chairs, this sumptuously decorated patisserie and *salon de thé* (tearoom), ideal for a sweet breakfast or a relaxing cup of afternoon tea, hasn't changed much since it was built in 1898. Size up the sweet offerings on display and tuck in.

Chez Paulette INTERNATIONAL €
(☑ 09 80 32 03 94; 44 rue des Cuisiniers; menus €10.50-15.50; ⊙ noon-6pm Tue & Wed, to 9.30pm Thu-Sat) This colourful cafe-restaurant throwback to the '60's is an enticing – and lovingly curated – jumble of Beatles-era wallpaper, old phones, crockery, polka-dot tablecloths, furniture, broken TVs and wall clocks. It's a fun addition to Bayeux and the food (a bit of a jumble as well, from fish and chips to soup, quiche and bagel sandwiches) is tops too. A small boutique conjoins it.

Au Ptit Bistrot MODERN FRENCH €€
(☑ 02 31 92 30 08; 31 rue Larcher; lunch menus €17-20, dinner menus €29-35, mains €18-22; ⊙ noon-2pm & 7-9pm Tue-Sat) Near the cathedral, this friendly, welcoming eatery whips up creative, beautifully prepared dishes that highlight the Norman bounty without pretension. Recent hits include braised beef cheek with red wine, polenta, grapefruit tapenade and vegetables or roasted pigeon with mushrooms and mashed parsnip. The kids menu is €11. Reservations essential.

L'Alchimie MODERN FRENCH €€
(☑ 02 31 92 30 08; 49 rue St-Jean; lunch menus €13-18; ⊙ noon-1.30pm & 7-10pm Mon- Wed, Fri & Sat, 7-10pm Thu) On a street lined with restaurants, L'Alchimie has a simple but elegant design that takes nothing from the beautifully presented dishes. Choose from the day's specials listed on a chalkboard menu, which might include *brandade de morue* (baked codfish pie) or *pastilla de poulet au gingembre et cumin* (chicken pastilla with ginger and cumin). Book ahead.

DON'T MISS

GET UP CLOSE

Cable-stayed bridge **Pont de Normandie** (car one-way €5.40), opened in 1995, stretches in a soaring 2km arch over the Seine between Le Havre and Honfleur. It's a typically French affair, as much sophisticated architecture as engineering, with two huge inverted-V-shaped columns holding aloft a delicate net of cables. Crossing it is quite a thrill – and the views of the Seine are magnificent. In each direction there's a narrow footpath and a bike lane.

La Rapière FRENCH €€
(📞 02 31 21 05 45; www.larapiere.net; 53 rue St-Jean; lunch menus €16-21, dinner menus €36-49, mains €20-28; ⊙ noon-1.30pm & 7-8.15pm Tue & Thu-Sat, 7-8.15pm Wed, closed mid-Dec–early Feb) Housed in a late-1400s mansion composed of stone walls and big wooden beams, this atmospheric restaurant specialises in Normandy staples such as terrines, duck and veal with Camembert. The various fixed-price *menus* assure a splendid meal on any budget.

ℹ️ Information

Tourist Office (📞 02 31 51 28 28; www.bayeux-bessin-tourisme.com; Pont St-Jean; ⊙ 9am-7pm Mon-Sat, 10am-1pm & 2-6pm Sun Jul & Aug, shorter hours rest of year)

ℹ️ Getting Around

Vélos (📞 02 31 92 89 16; www.velosbayeux.com; 5 rue Larcher; adult bike per half-/full day from €7.50/10, child bike per half-/full day from €7.50/5; ⊙ 8am-8.30pm) Year-round bike rental from a fruit and veggie store a few paces from the tourist office.

D-Day Beaches

🖝 Tours

Accessible and handy introductions to the beaches, guided minibus tours – lots of local companies offer them – can be an excellent way to get a sense of the D-Day beaches and their place in history. The Bayeux tourist office can handle reservations or book online for Caen.

Tours by Le Mémorial – Un Musée pour la Paix BUS
(📞 02 31 06 06 45; www.memorial-caen.fr; tours with/without lunch €131/95; ⊙ tours 1pm, closed 3 weeks in Jan) Excellent year-round minibus

---

THE BATTLE OF NORMANDY

In early 1944, an Allied invasion of continental Europe seemed inevitable. Hitler's disastrous campaign on the Russian front and the Luftwaffe's inability to control the skies over Europe had left Germany vulnerable. Both sides knew a landing was coming – the only questions were where and, of course, when.

Several sites were considered by Allied command. After long deliberation, it was decided that the beaches along Normandy's northern coast – rather than the even more heavily fortified coastline further north around Calais, where Hitler was expecting an attack – would serve as a surprise spearhead into occupied Europe.

Code-named 'Operation Overlord', the invasion began on the night of 5 June 1944 when three paratroop divisions were dropped behind enemy lines. At about 6.30am on the morning of 6 June, six amphibious divisions stormed ashore at five beaches, backed up by an unimaginable 6000 sea craft and 13,000 aeroplanes. The initial landing force involved some 45,000 troops; 15 more divisions were to follow once successful beachheads had been established.

The narrow Straits of Dover had seemed the most likely invasion spot to the Germans, who'd set about heavily reinforcing the area around Calais and the other Channel ports. Allied intelligence went to extraordinary lengths to encourage the German belief that the invasion would be launched north of Normandy: double agents, leaked documents and fake radio traffic, buttressed by phony airfields and an entirely fictitious American army group, supposedly stationed in southeast England, all suggested the invasion would centre on the Pas de Calais.

Because of the tides and unpredictable weather patterns, Allied planners had only a few dates available each month in which to launch the invasion. On 5 June, the date chosen, the worst storm in 20 years set in, delaying the operation. The weather had improved only marginally the next day, but General Dwight D Eisenhower, Allied commander-in-chief, gave the go-ahead: 6 June would be D-Day.

In the hours leading up to D-Day, French Resistance units set about disrupting German communications. Just after midnight on 6 June, the first Allied troops were on French soil. British commandos and glider units captured key bridges and destroyed German gun emplacements, and the American 82nd and 101st Airborne Divisions landed west of the invasion site. Although the paratroops' tactical victories were few, they caused confusion in German ranks and, because of their relatively small numbers, the German high command was convinced that the real invasion had not yet begun.

The Battle of Normandy

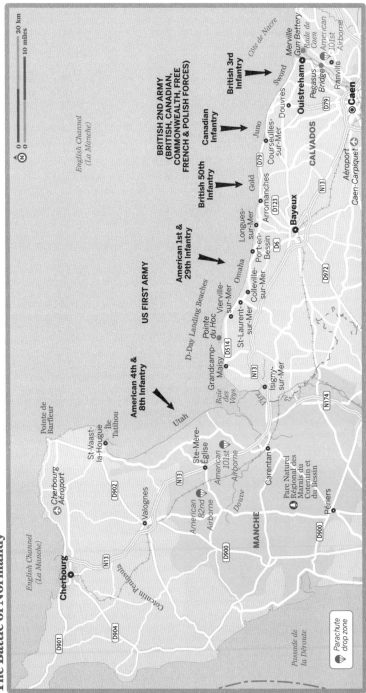

tours (four to five hours) depart at 1pm, to take in Pointe du Hoc, Omaha Beach, the American cemetery and the artificial British harbour at Arromanches. There are cheaper tours in full-size buses from June to August. Rates include entry to Le Mémorial – Un Musée pour la Paix. There's a choice of two tours, one including lunch.

Normandy Sightseeing Tours TOURS
(📞 02 31 51 70 52; www.normandy-sightseeing-tours.com; 6 rue St-Jean, Bayeux; adult/child morning €60/40, full-day €100/60) This experienced Bayeux-based outfit offers informative morning tours of the various D-Day beaches and cemeteries, as well as all-day excursions. Check the website for further details.

Normandy Tours TOURS
(📞 02 31 92 10 70; www.normandy-landing-tours.com; 26 place de la Gare, Bayeux; adult/student €72/62) Offers well-regarded four- to five-hour tours of the main sites starting at 8.15am and 1.15pm on most days, as well as personally tailored trips. Based at Bayeux's Hôtel de la Gare, facing the train station.

Omaha Beach

The most brutal fighting on D-Day took place on the 7km stretch of coastline around Vierville-sur-Mer, St-Laurent-sur-Mer and Colleville-sur-Mer, 15km northwest of Bayeux, known as 'Bloody Omaha' to US veterans. More than seven decades on, little evidence of the carnage unleashed here on 6 June 1944 remains, except for the harrowing American cemetery and concrete German bunkers, though at very low tide you can see a few remnants of the Mulberry Harbour.

These days Omaha is a peaceful place, a beautiful stretch of fine golden sand partly lined with dunes and summer homes. Circuit de la Plage d'Omaha, trail-marked with a yellow stripe, is a self-guided tour along the beach.

◎ Sights

Normandy American Cemetery & Memorial MEMORIAL
(p22)

Overlord Museum MUSEUM
(📞 02 31 22 00 55; www.overlordmuseum.com; D514, Colleville-sur-Mer; adult/child €7.80/5.70; ⏱ 10am-5.30pm mid-Feb–Mar, Oct & Nov, to 6.30pm Apr, May & Sep, 9.30am-7pm Jun-Aug, closed Jan–mid-Feb) This excellent museum has an astonishing collection of restored WWII military equipment from both sides; the human dimension of the war is brought movingly to life with photos, audio clips, letters and personal stories and recollections. The museum is situated just up the hill from the Normandy American Cemetery & Memorial. You could easily spend a few hours here, so plan your visit accordingly as you will need time for both the museum and the cemetery.

Arromanches-les-Bains

Today, Arromanches-les-Bains is an important D-Day stop for the remains of the Mulberry Harbours caissons visible in the waters and the exhibits at the Musée du Débarquement, dedicated to the history of the artificial harbours and their significance in the war effort.

◎ Sights

Mulberry Harbours Caissons RUINS
The harbour established at Omaha was completely destroyed by a ferocious gale (the worst storm to lash the Normandy coast in four decades) just two weeks after D-Day, but the impressive remains of three dozen caissons belonging to the second, Port Winston (named after Churchill), can still be seen off Arromanches-les-Bains, 10km northeast of Bayeux. At low tide you

Gun emplacement, Omaha Beach

can even walk out to one of the caissons from the beach, but they are being gradually eroded by the sea.

Arromanches 360°
Circular Cinema   THEATRE
(☑ 02 31 06 06 44; www.arromanches360. com; chemin du Calvaire; adult/child €6/5.50; ⊙ 10am-between 5pm & 6pm, from 9.30am May-Aug, closed 3 weeks in Jan & Mon mid-Nov–mid-Feb) The best view of Port Winston and nearby Gold Beach is from the hill east of town, site of the popular Arromanches 360° Circular Cinema, which screens archival footage of the Battle of Normandy every half-hour (on the hour and at half past the hour); it is run by Caen's Le Mémorial – Un Musée pour la Paix (p18). Entrance is free for WWII veterans. Check the website for details of guided tours (adult/child €2.50/2), held at noon and 4pm.

Musée du Débarquement   MUSEUM
(p21)

Juno Beach

Dune-lined Juno Beach, 12km east of Arromanches around Courseulles-sur-Mer, was stormed by Canadian troops on D-Day. A Cross of Lorraine marks the spot where General Charles de Gaulle came ashore shortly after the landings. He was followed by Winston Churchill on 12 June and King George VI on 16 June. A bunker is by the beach, which can be accessed on tours, led by the Juno Beach Centre.

◉ Sights

Juno Beach Centre   MUSEUM
(p20)

Bény-sur-Mer Canadian War
Cemetery   CEMETERY
(www.cwgc.org; D35) The Bény-sur-Mer Canadian War Cemetery is 4km south of Courseulles-sur-Mer near Reviers.

Longues-sur-Mer

Part of the Nazis' Atlantic Wall, the massive concrete casemates and 150mm German guns at Longues-sur-Mer, 6km west of Arromanches, were designed to hit targets some 20km away, including both Gold Beach (to the east) and Omaha Beach (to the west). Seven and a half decades after their installation, the guns and their stolid concrete

Église St-Étienne (p71), Caen
S74/SHUTTERSTOCK ©

casemates survive and constitute one of the highlights along the coast. In their now silent and disused form, they serve as a fitting testament to the collapse of the German occupation.

❶ Information

Longues Tourist Office (☑ 02 31 21 46 87; www.bayeux-bessin-tourisme.com; Site de la Batterie; ⊙ 10am-1pm & 2-6pm, closed Nov-Mar) Has details on guided tours (adult/child €5/3) to the German artillery batteries at Longues-sur-Mer, available on weekends from April to October (and daily in July and August). View the excellent website for a full list of events in the region.

Caen

POP 109,300
Founded by William the Conqueror in the 11th century, Caen – capital of the Basse Normandie region – was massively damaged during the 1944 Battle of Normandy, but considerable history and heritage survives to make it a very good-looking city, especially in its central areas. Visitors will discover the imposing bastions of a superb medieval château, two ancient abbeys and a clutch of excellent museums, including an outstanding and enthralling museum of war and peace, largely dedicated to D-Day, WWII and its aftermath. With its decent hotels, superb collection of restaurants, atmospheric streets

Caen

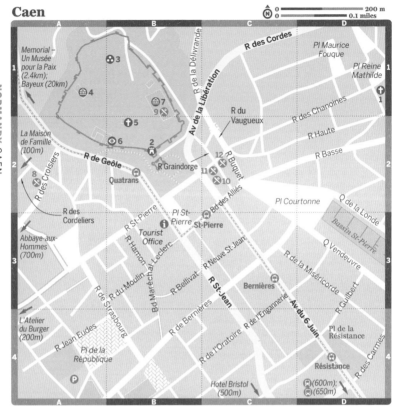

Caen

⊙ Sights
1 Abbaye-aux-Dames D1
2 Château de Caen B2
3 Donjon B1
4 Échiquier A1
5 Église St-Georges B2
6 Jardin des Simples B2
7 Musée des Beaux-Arts B1

⊗ Eating
8 À Contre Sens A2
9 Café Mancel B1
10 Dolly's C2
11 Dolly's 2 Go C2
12 Le Bouchon du Vaugueux C2

and manageable size, Caen is a terrific place to explore; the easygoing city is also a launchpad to the nearby D-Day sights spread out along the coast.

⊙ Sights

Le Mémorial – Un Musée pour la Paix MUSEUM
(p18)

Château de Caen CHATEAU
(www.musee-de-normandie.caen.fr; ⊙8am-10pm; ⓟ) FREE Looming above the centre of the city, Caen's magnificent castle walls – massive battlements overlooking a now dry moat – were established by William the Conqueror, Duke of Normandy, in 1060. Visitors can walk around the ramparts and visit the 12th-century **Église St-Georges**, which holds an information centre with a diorama of the castle, and the **Échiquier** (Exchequer; ☑02 31 30 47 60), which dates from about 1100 and is one of the oldest civic buildings in Normandy. The castle affords splendid visuals over the town at sunset.

The Jardin des Simples is a garden of medicinal and aromatic herbs cultivated during the Middle Ages, some of them poisonous. There are also two worthwhile museums in the castle grounds, and a good restaurant-cafe. The mighty 12th-century donjon (keep) only survives today as vestiges and foundations. Tours of the castle are provided by the tourist office (p72) during summer, but only in French.

Musée des Beaux-Arts GALLERY
(Fine Arts Museum; ☑ 02 31 30 47 70; www.mba. caen.fr; Château de Caen; adult/child €3.50/ free, incl temporary exhibition €5.50; ⊙ 9.30am-12.30pm & 2-6pm Mon-Fri, 11am-6pm Sat & Sun Jun-Oct, 9.30am-12.30pm & 2-6pm Wed-Fri, 11am-6pm Sat & Sun Nov-May) This excellent and well-curated museum takes you on a tour through the history of Western art from the 15th to 21st centuries, including works depicting landscapes and interiors found around Normandy. The collection includes works by Rubens, Tintoretto, Géricault, Monet, Bonnard, Boudin, Dufy and Courbet, among many others. Situated inside the Château de Caen.

Abbaye-aux-Hommes ABBEY
(Abbaye-St-Étienne; ☑ 02 31 30 42 81; rue Guillaume le Conquérant; church free, cloisters €2; ⊙ church 9.30am-1pm & 2-7pm Mon-Sat, 2-6.30pm Sun, cloister 8.30am-5pm Mon-Fri, 9.30am-1pm & 2-5.30pm Sat & most Sun) Caen's most important medieval site is the Men's Abbey – now city hall – and, right next door, the magnificent, multi-turreted Église St-Étienne (St Stephen's Church), with its Romanesque nave, Gothic choir and William the Conqueror's tomb (rebuilt; the original was destroyed by a 16th-century Calvinist mob and, in 1793, by fevered revolutionaries).

The complex is 1km southwest of the Château de Caen; to get there by car, follow the signs to the 'Hôtel de Ville'.

Abbaye-aux-Dames ABBEY
(Abbaye-de-la-Trinité; ☑ 02 31 06 98 98; place Reine Mathilde) Highlights at the Women's Abbey complex in the east of the town centre, once run by the Benedictines, include Église de la Trinité – look for Matilda's tomb behind the main altar and the striking pink stained-glass windows just beyond. Free tours (at 2.30pm and 4pm daily) take you through the interior, but you can snoop around the courtyard and the church on your own at other times, except during Mass.

CAEN DAY TRIPPER

The new, highly informative and timely (for the 75th anniversary of D-Day) **Civilians in Wartime Memorial** (☑ 02 31 06 06 45; www.memorial-falaise. fr; Falaise; adult/child €7.50/6.50; ⊙ 10am-5.30pm Feb-Oct) in the town of Falaise, 41km southeast of Caen, gets you under the skin of being a civilian during the battle of Normandy. The life of civilians in the conflict is brought into stark relief through relics and artefacts of war, the stories of survivors, interactive tablets and a film that reveals the horror of the conflict and its aftermath. The museum is located near the Château de Falaise.

A €28 ticket includes the Civilians in Wartime Memorial, Le Mémorial – Un Musée pour la Paix in Caen and the Arromanches 360° Circular Cinema.

1944 Radar Museum MUSEUM
(☑ 02 31 06 06 45; www.musee.radar.fr; rte de Basly, Douvres-la-Délivrande; adult/child €5.50/ free; ⊙ 10am-6pm Tue-Sun May–mid-Sep) Located 5km north of Caen within two restored German bunkers (bunker H 622 and bunker L 479), this museum is interesting for anyone of a technical bent or those who wish to understand more about the role of radar in WWII. You can see a large German *Würzburg* radar antenna as well as three other radars in what was one of the most important German radar stations in Normandy. The site was captured by British forces on 17 June 1944.

🛏 Sleeping

Hotel Bristol HOTEL €
(☑ 02 31 84 59 76; www.hotelbristolcaen.com; 31 rue du 11 Novembre; s/d from €75/85; 🛜) The centrally located Hotel Bristol has well-maintained contemporary, rather neutrally toned rooms with comfortable beds and huge windows. It's the friendly and welcoming service, however, that really sets this place apart from other similarly priced options. Breakfast is €9.50; parking is €10 per night.

⭐ **La Maison de Famille** B&B €€
(☑ 06 61 64 88 54; www.maisondefamille.sitew. com; 4 rue Elie de Beaumont; d/ste €75/105; 🅿 🛜)

This grand and adorable four-room B&B, overflowing with personality, charm and history (it dates to the 17th century), occupies three floors of an imposing townhouse. Added perks include a lovely breakfast in a fine dining room, private parking and a marvellous staircase. The attic apartment is atmospheric, while the suite has access to the peaceful garden.

Eating

Dolly's
CAFE €

(☑02 31 94 03 29; 16-18 av de la Libération; mains from €9; ☺11am-11pm Tue, 10am-11pm Wed & Sun, 10am-1am Thu-Sat; 🐟) This colourful British-style cafe is popular and often full, so it can be a bit of a struggle to get a seat, but it's the place for greasy fry-up brekkies, burgers, fish and chips (€13.50), plus salads and healthier fare for the body-conscious and vegetarians. Service is brusque. If it's too full of elbows, a smaller **takeout branch** (☑02 50 54 23 23; 18 rue Montoir-Poissonnerie; ☺11am-7.30pm Tue-Thu, to 11pm Fri & Sat; 🖉) is nearby.

L'Atelier du Burger
BURGERS €

(☑02 31 50 13 44; www.latelier-duburger.fr; 27 rue Écuyère; mains €7.50-9; ☺noon-2.30pm & 7-11.30pm; 🐟) Near the end of bar-lined rue Écuyère, this place does a busy trade in juicy, thick burgers piled high with guacamole, grilled onions and other toppings. The burgers are truly top-form, and so are the chips. It's an informal and relaxed place: order at the counter, grab your own drink, and take a seat in the stone-walled back room or on the small terrace.

Café Mancel
FRENCH €€

(☑02 31 86 63 64; www.cafemancel.com; Château de Caen; menus €18-25; ☺noon-10pm Tue-Sat, to 2pm Sun) In the same building as the Musée des Beaux-Arts within the Château de Caen, this stylish place serves up delicious, traditional French cuisine – everything from pan-fried Norman-style beefsteak to hearty Caen-style *tripes*, delivered by attentive staff. There's a lovely sun terrace, which also makes a fine spot for a drink outside of busy meal times.

Le Bouchon du Vaugueux
FRENCH €€

(☑02 31 44 26 26; www.bouchonduvaugueux.com; 12 rue Graindorge; lunch menus €17-25, dinner menus €23-35; ☺noon-2pm & 7-10pm Tue-Sat; 🖭) The giant wine cork marks the spot at this tiny *bistrot gourmande* (gour-met bistro), which matches creative modern cooking with a first-rate wine selection (from €4 a glass), sourced from small producers all over France. Staff are happy to translate the chalkboard menu and there's a kids menu too (€9). Reservations recommended.

À Contre Sens
MODERN FRENCH €€

(☑02 31 97 44 48; www.acontresenscaen.fr/a-con tre-sens; 8 rue des Croisiers; mains €30-38, menus €26-56; ☺noon-1.15pm & 7.30-9.15pm Wed-Sat, 7.30-9.15pm Tue) À Contre Sens' stylish interior and serene atmosphere belie the hotbed of seething creativity happening in the kitchen. Under the helm of chef Anthony Caillot, meals are thoughtfully crafted and superbly presented. Expect dishes such as seaweed risotto with apple and coriander or veal rubbed with herbs, endive and ham.

ℹ Information

Tourist Office (☑02 31 27 14 14; www.caen-tourisme.fr; 12 place St-Pierre; ☺9.30am-6.30pm Mon-Sat, 9.30am-1.30pm Sun Apr-Sep, 9.30am-1pm & 2-6pm Mon-Sat Oct-Feb, to 6.30pm Mar)

Deauville

POP 3800

Good-looking and chic Deauville has been a playground of well-heeled Parisians ever since it was founded by Napoléon III's half-brother, the Duke of Morny, in 1861. Expensive, flashy and brash, it's packed with designer boutiques, deluxe hotels and meticulously tended public gardens, and hosts two racetracks (Deauville-La Touques Racecourse and Deauville-Clairefontaine Racecourse) and the high-profile Deauville American Film Festival.

The port town is 15km southwest of Honfleur, separated from equally popular Trouville-sur-Mer by the River Touques, which flows into the sea here. Deauville is hugely popular with denizens of Paris, who flock here year-round on weekends – and all week long from June to September and during Paris' school holidays.

🏃 Activities

The rich and beautiful strut their stuff along the beachside **Promenade des Planches**, a 643m-long boardwalk that's lined with a row of 1920s cabins named after famous Americans (mainly film stars). After swimming

Deauville

in the nearby 50m **Piscine Olympique** (Olympic swimming pool; ☑ 02 31 14 02 17; bd de la Mer, Deauville; weekday/weekend from €4/6; ⊘ 10am-2pm & 3.30-7pm Mon-Sat, 9am-4pm Sun, closed 2 weeks in Jan & 3 weeks in Jun), filled with seawater heated to 28°C, locals – like you – can head to the beach, hundreds of metres wide at low tide; walk across the street to their eye-popping, neo-something mansion; or head down the block to the spectacularly Italianate casino.

✷ Festivals & Events

Deauville American Film Festival FILM (www.festival-deauville.com; ⊘ Sep) Deauville has a fair bit of Beverly Hills glitz and glamour so it's an appropriate venue for an annual festival celebrating American cinema, running since 1975. Held for 10 days from early September; tickets cost €35 for one day or €160 for the whole festival. Students to the age of 26 can get tickets for one day/ whole festival for €16/110.

🛏 Sleeping & Eating

There's not a great selection of hotels in Deauville – there's a superior selection in Trouville-sur-Mer next door. Prices are highest and reservations are recommended in July and August, and year-round on weekends and holidays; and lowest (we're talking half off) from October to Easter, except during Paris' school holidays, and most of the year on weekdays.

L'Essentiel FUSION €€ (☑ 02 31 87 22 11; 29 rue Mirabeau; lunch menus €27-32, dinner menus €69, mains €31-39; ⊘ noon-2pm & 7.30-11pm Thu-Mon) One of Deauville's top dining rooms, L'Essentiel serves up an imaginative blend of French ingredients with Asian and Latin American accents. Start off with codfish croquettes with sweet potato aioli before moving on to scallops with broccoli yuzu, or wagyu flank steak with roasted turnips and smoked cashew juice.

Le Comptoir et la Table MODERN FRENCH €€€ (☑ 02 31 88 92 51; www.lecomptoiretlatable. fr; 1 quai de la Marine, Deauville; mains €28-42; ⊘ noon-2.30pm & 7-10.30pm Thu-Tue) Seasonal ingredients fresh from the market are transformed into delicious dishes, some of Italian inspiration, served in appealingly maritime surroundings. Specialities include risotto with cream of truffles and scallops, and grilled lobster. A further plus is the attentive service. You can find Le Comptoir et la Table along the waterfront, about four blocks northwest of the Deauville-Trouville bridge.

ℹ Information

Deauville Tourist Office (☑ 02 31 14 40 00; www.indeauville.fr; quai de la Gare; ⊘ 10am-6pm Mon-Sat, 10am-1pm & 2-5pm Sun)

Trouville-sur-Mer

POP 4800

Unpretentious Trouville-sur-Mer – usually known simply as Trouville – is both a veteran beach resort, graced with impressive mansions from the late 1800s, and a working fishing port. Popular with middle-class French families, the town was frequented by painters and writers during the 19th century (eg Mozin and Flaubert), lured by the 2km-long sandy beach and the laid-back seaside ambience.

The port town is right next to Deauville and is similarly very popular with Parisians, who descend on Trouville-sur-Mer at weekends and during the summer, vastly swelling the population.

◎ Sights & Activities

Trouville has a waterfront casino, a wide beach and a **Promenade des Planches** (boardwalk). At the latter, 583m long and outfitted with Bauhaus-style pavilions from the 1930s, you can swim in a freshwater swimming pool and windsurf; there's also a playground for kids. Trouville's most impressive 19th-century villas are right nearby.

Musée Villa Montabello   MUSEUM
(☑ 02 31 88 16 26; 64 rue du Général Leclerc; adult/child €3/free, Sun free; ◎2-5.30pm Wed-Mon Apr–mid-Nov, from 11am Sat, Sun & holidays) In a grand mansion dating to 1865, this munici-pal museum recounts Trouville's history and features works by Charles Mozin, Eugène Isabey and Charles Pecrus. The Musée Villa Montabello is situated 1km northeast of the tourist office, near the beach (and signed off the beach). The two towns and beach scenes of Trouville and Deauville play a starring role in the impressionist works in the small permanent collection.

🛏 Sleeping

La Maison Normande   HOTEL €
(☑ 02 31 88 12 25; www.la-maison-normande.com; 4 place de Lattre de Tassigny; d €55-85; 🛜) The 17 rooms in this late-17th-century half-timbered Norman house vary considerably in size and style and are eminently serviceable, offering very good value indeed. Prices rise slightly a bit on Friday and Saturday. Breakfast is €8.50.

Le Flaubert   HOTEL €€
(☑ 02 31 88 37 23; www.flaubert.fr; rue Gustave Flaubert; d incl breakfast €129-179, ste €199-299; 🛜) With a fresh and breezy seafront perspective and lovely, bright accommodation, Le Flaubert is a peach. Each room has its own personality, with ample wood, wicker chairs and the occasional pastel shade, but it's the position right by the beach that seals it. Sea-view rooms go like hot cakes, so book early in summer. Parking is €12 per day.

ANTON_IVANOV/SHUTTERSTOCK ©

Trouville-sur-Mer

Le Fer à Cheval

HOTEL €€

(☑ 02 31 98 30 20; www.hotel-trouville.com; 11 rue Victor Hugo; s €64-80, d €92-105, ste from €170; ⚡) Ensconced in three beautiful turn-of-the-20th-century buildings, this very welcoming 34-room hotel has comfortable, modern rooms with big double-glazed windows, stylish decor and bright bathrooms. It's situated two short blocks inland from the riverfront. Breakfast is either a buffet in the breakfast room or a continental version served in your room. Prices rise on Fridays and Saturdays.

✗ Eating

There are lots of restaurants and buzzing brasseries along riverfront bd Fernand Moureaux; many specialise in fresh fish, mussels and seafood. The area has a fantastic atmosphere on summer evenings. Inland, check out the small restaurants and cafes along and near rue d'Orléans and on pedestrianised rue des Bains.

Marché aux Poissons

SEAFOOD €

(Fish Market; bd Fernand Moureaux; ⊙ 8am-7.30pm) The sizeable Marché aux Poissons is *the* place in Trouville to head for fresh oysters with lemon (from €9 to €16 a dozen) and other maritime delicacies. Even if you don't have access to a kitchen, there's cooked peel-and-eat shrimp, mussels, sea urchins and scallops, to enjoy at a table out front. Located on the waterfront 250m south of the casino.

Les Vapeurs

BRASSERIE €€

(☑ 02 31 88 15 24; 160 bd Fernand Moureaux; mains €18-38; ⊙ noon-11.30pm) Across from the fish market, Les Vapeurs has been going strong in Trouville since 1927. The huge menu is a showcase for seafood platters, oysters (from €15 for six), mussels in cream sauce, grilled haddock, lobster and classic brasserie fare (like steak tartare). It's served amid an old-time ambience, with black-and-white photos, a touch of neon and wicker chairs at the outdoor tables in front. There are dishes for the young ones too.

Tivoli Bistro

BISTRO €€

(☑ 02 31 98 43 44; 27 rue Charles Mozin; menus €30; ⊙ 12.15-2pm & 7.15-9.30pm Fri-Tue) You won't find a cosier place in Trouville than this much-loved hideaway, tucked away on a narrow side street a block inland from the riverfront. It's famous for its delicious *sole meunière* (Dover sole; €32.50) and exqui-site homemade terrine, or you can just stop by for a quick serving of delicious *moules marinière* (mussels; €12).

ⓘ Information

Trouville Tourist Office (☑ 02 31 14 60 70; www.trouvillesurmer.org; 32 bd Fernand Moureaux; ⊙ 10am-6pm Mon-Sat, to 1.30pm Sun Sep-Jun, 9.30am-7pm Mon-Sat, 10am-6pm Sun Jul & Aug) Has a free map of Trouville and sells map-brochures for two self-guided architectural tours (€4) of town and also two rural walks (€1).

Honfleur

POP 8200

Long a favourite with painters such as Monet, Normandy's most charming port town is a popular day-trip destination for Parisian families. Though the centre can be overrun with visitors on warm weekends and in summer, it's hard not to love the rugged maritime charm of the Vieux Bassin (Old Harbour), which evokes maritime Normandy of centuries past.

In the 16th and 17th centuries, Honfleur was one of France's most important ports for commerce and exploration. Some of the earliest French expeditions to Brazil and Newfoundland began here, and in 1608, Samuel de Champlain set sail from Honfleur to found Québec City.

◉ Sights

Honfleur is spread around the roughly rectangular Vieux Bassin and, along its southeast side, the Enclos, the once-walled old town. Église Ste-Catherine is northwest of the Vieux Bassin (up the hill).

Honfleur is superb for aimless ambling, especially if you have a walking map from the tourist office. One option is to head north from the Lieutenance along quai des Passagers to **Jetée de l'Ouest** (Western Jetty), which forms the west side of the Avant Port, out to the broad mouth of the Seine. Possible stops include the **Jardin des Personnalités**, a park featuring figures from Honfleur history; the beach; and **Naturospace** (☑ 02 31 81 77 00; www.naturospace.com; bd Charles V; adult/child €9/7; ⊙ 10am-5pm Feb-Mar & Oct–mid-Nov, to 6.30pm Apr-Sep), a lush greenhouse filled with free-flying tropical butterflies and birds that's situated 500m northwest of the Lieutenance.

CAMEMBERT COUNTRY

Some of the most enduring names in the pungent world of French *fromage* come from Normandy, including **Pont L'Évêque**, **Livarot** and, most famous of all, **Camembert**, all of which are named after towns south of Honfleur, on or near the D579.

It's thought that monks first began experimenting with cheesemaking in the Pays d'Auge area of Normandy sometime in the 11th century, but the present-day varieties didn't emerge until around the 17th century. The invention of Camembert is generally credited to Marie Harel, who was supposedly given the secret of soft cheesemaking by an abbot from Brie on the run from revolutionary mobs in 1790. Whatever the truth of the legend, the cheese was a huge success at the local market in Vimoutiers, and the *fabrication* of Camembert quickly grew from cottage production into a veritable industry. The distinctive round wooden boxes, in which Camembert is wrapped, have been around since 1890; they were designed by a local engineer to protect the soft disc of cheese during its bruising long-distance travel.

If you're interested in seeing how the cheese is made, you can take a tour of Maison du Camembert (p34), an early-19th-century farm restored by Président, one of the largest Camembert producers. It's in the centre of the town of Camembert, about 60km south of Honfleur.

The tourist office also has audioguides (€5; in English, French and German) for a 1½-hour walking tour of the town.

Le Pass Musées (adult €13) gets you into all four municipal museums for less than the price of two.

Vieux Bassin   HISTORIC SITE
The old harbour, with its bobbing pleasure boats, is Honfleur's focal point. On the west side, quai Ste-Catherine is lined with tall, taper-thin houses – many protected from the elements by slate tiles – dating from the 16th to 18th centuries. The **Lieutenance** (12 place Ste-Catherine), at the mouth of the old harbour, was once the residence of the town's royal governor. Just northeast of the Lieutenance is the **Avant Port**, home to Honfleur's dozen fishing vessels, which sell their catch at the **Marché au Poisson** (Fish Market; Jetée de Transit; ⊙ 8am-noon or later Thu-Sun).

Small children will get a kick out of a ride on the carousel, situated opposite the Lieutenance.

Église Ste-Catherine   CHURCH
(p38)

★ **Les Maisons Satie**   MUSEUM
(🎧 02 31 89 11 11; www.musees-honfleur.fr/maison-satie.html; 67 bd Charles V & 90 rue Haute; adult/child €6.20/free; ⊙ 10am-7pm Wed-Mon May-Sep, 11am-6pm Wed-Mon Oct-Apr) This unusual and intriguing complex captures the whimsical spirit of the eccentric avant-garde compos-er Erik Satie (1866–1925), who lived and worked in Honfleur and was born in one of the two half-timbered *maisons Satie* (Satie houses). Visitors wander through the beguiling rooms, each concealing a surreal surprise, as a headset plays Satie's strangely familiar music. Les Maisons Satie is situated 350m northwest of the northern end of the Vieux Bassin.

Musée Eugène Boudin   GALLERY
(🎧 02 31 89 54 00; www.musees-honfleur.fr; 50 rue de l'Homme de Bois; adult/child Jun-Oct €8/free, Nov-May €6/free; ⊙ 10am-1pm & 2-6pm Wed-Mon Jun-Oct, 2.30-5.30pm Wed-Mon, 10am-noon Sat & Sun Nov-May) This museum features superb 19th- and 20th-century paintings of Normandy's towns and coast, including works by Dubourg, Dufy and Monet. One room is devoted to Eugène Boudin, an early impressionist and marine painter (he was the son of a sailor), who was born in Honfleur in 1824 and whom Baudelaire called the 'king of skies' for his luscious skyscapes.

Musée d'Ethnographie
et d'Art Populaire Normand   MUSEUM
(🎧 02 31 89 14 12; www.musees-honfleur.fr; rue de la Prison; adult/child €4.20/free, incl Musée de la Marine €5.30/free; ⊙ 10am-noon & 2-6.30pm Tue-Sun Apr-Sep, 2.30-5.30pm Tue-Fri, 10am-noon & 2.30-5.30pm Sat & Sun mid-Feb–Mar & Oct-late Nov, closed late Nov–mid-Feb) Through multiple rooms, this museum gathers together exhibits on domestic and economic life in

16th- to 19th-century Normandy, portraying traditional costumes, furniture and housewares. It's located in two adjacent 16th-century buildings: a one-time prison and a house, hence the name of the street. A €13 pass is available for access to Musée d'Ethnographie et d'Art Populaire Normand, Musée Eugène Boudin and the **Musée de la Marine** (quai St-Étienne; adult/child €4.20/free, incl Musée d'Ethnographie €5.30/free; ⊘10am-noon & 2-6.30pm Tue-Sun Apr-Sep, 2.30-5.30pm Tue-Fri, 10am-noon Sat & Sun mid-Feb–Mar, Oct & Nov, closed Dec–mid-Feb).

🛏 Sleeping

Hôtel Monet   HOTEL €
(☑02 31 89 00 90; www.hotel-monet-honfleur.com; rue Charriere du Puits; incl breakfast d/f from €65/100; P🛜) Up the hill, out of the action and run by welcoming Sylvie and Christophe, this delightful and small hotel has modern, neat rooms with a sweet, small cafe in the lobby. All rooms come with terrace; breakfast is served either in your room or on your terrace.

⭐**La Petite Folie**   B&B €€
(☑06 74 39 46 46; www.lapetitefolie-honfleur.com; 44 rue Haute; d incl breakfast €145-195, apt €195-275; 🛜) Penny Vincent, an American who moved to France from San Francisco, and her French husband Thierry are the gracious hosts at this elegant home, built in 1830 and still adorned by the original stained glass and tile floors. Each room has a different design, with original artwork, and the best are filled with vintage furnishings and overlook the pretty garden.

La Cour Ste-Catherine   BOUTIQUE HOTEL €€
(☑02 31 89 42 40; www.coursaintecatherine.com; 74 rue du Puits; r €120, ste €120-150, apt €150-200; 🛜) With a lovely courtyard garden that flowers with tulips and *Magnolia grandiflora,* this charming and tranquil place has adorable rooms, some charmingly tucked away under the eaves of the garret. There are six rooms and two apartments in all, with breakfast included.

Le Fond de la Cour   B&B €€
(☑06 72 20 72 98; www.lefonddelacour.com; 29 rue Eugène Boudin; d €99-150, cottage from €145; 🛜) Watched over by a dog, a cat and some chickens, rooms here (including a studio and a cottage, which sleeps up to four) are light, airy and immaculate. The energetic Amanda, a native of Scotland, goes to great lengths to make you feel at home. Breakfast, with eggs, croissants, crêpes, bread and Normandy cheese, is included in all room rates.

À l'École Buissonnière   B&B €€
(☑06 16 18 43 62; www.a-lecole-buissonniere.com; 4 rue de la Foulerie; d/ste from €100/120; 🛜) Occupying a former girls' school built in the 1600s, this handsomely restored

Honfleur

Bistro des Artistes, Honfleur

B&B has five luxurious rooms with antique wood furnishings, some with terrace for sun-catching. For lunch, stop by the *bar à fromages* (cheese bar), or ask your hosts to prepare a picnic lunch (€25). Guests can also borrow a bike (no charge). Parking is €10 per night.

La Maison de Lucie
BOUTIQUE HOTEL €€€

(☑02 31 14 40 40; www.lamaisondelucie.com; 44 rue des Capucins; s/d €170/200, ste €250-330; P🛜) This marvellous and intimate nine-room, three-suite hideaway is a gem. Some bedrooms, panelled in oak, have Moroccan-tile bathrooms and fantastic views across the harbour to the Pont de Normandie. The shady terrace is a glorious place for a summer breakfast. A chic jacuzzi-spa (€40 for two people, 45 minutes) in the old brick-vaulted cellar rounds it off. No lift.

🍴 Eating

Marché
MARKET €

(place Ste-Catherine; ⏱9am-noon Wed & Sat) A traditional food market on Saturday, a *biologique* (organic) market on Wednesday. There's usually a vendor selling made-to-order crêpes. The market is next to Église Ste-Catherine.

La Cidrerie
CRÊPES €

(☑02 31 89 59 85; 26 place Hamelin; mains €8-12; ⏱noon-2.30pm & 7-9.30pm Thu-Mon) For an inexpensive and casual meal, La Cidrerie is a superb choice, serving up a winning combination of piping-hot *galettes* (savoury buckwheat crêpes) and fizzy Norman ciders served in bowls. You can choose from over a dozen savoury options, then finish with a dessert crêpe (try one with homemade caramel sauce). There's also warm cider – perfect if (when) the weather sours.

Bistro des Artistes
FRENCH €€

(☑02 31 89 95 90; 14 place Berthelot; mains €20-28; ⏱noon-2.30pm & 7-9.30pm Thu-Tue) This small and dainty eatery near Église Ste-Catherine is managed by Anne-Marie Carneiro, who greets guests, waits tables and cooks. Service can therefore be a bit slow, but dishes are magnificent, and everything is made in-house, including the hearty bread brought to your table. The menu – on a chalkboard – changes frequently, but features beautifully turned-out dishes.

L'Endroit
FRENCH €€

(☑02 31 88 08 43; www.restaurantlendroit honfleur.com; 3 rue Charles et Paul Bréard; weekday lunch menus €25.50, other menus €32.50, mains €24-26; ⏱noon-1.30pm & 7.30-9pm Wed-Fri, noon-2pm & 7.30-10pm Sat, noon-2pm & 7.30-9.30pm Sun; 🛜) In an eclectic and artfully designed space with an open kitchen, L'Endroit serves beautifully prepared dishes that showcase the bounty of Normandy fields and coastline. The menu is brief, with just a few roasted meats and seafood dishes on offer, but the high-quality cooking, friendly service and appealing surrounds (including a secret roof terrace for smokers) wins plaudits.

★ La Fleur de Sel
GASTRONOMY €€€

(☑ 02 31 89 01 92; www.lafleurdesel-honfleur.com; 17 rue Haute; menus €32-62; ⊙ noon-1.30pm & 7.15-9pm Wed-Sun) Honfleur-raised Vincent Guyon cooked in some of Paris' top kitchens before returning to his hometown to make good and open his own (now celebrated) restaurant. Guyon uses the highest-quality locally sourced ingredients and plenty of invention (with roast meats and wild-caught seafood featuring ginger and kaffir-lime vinaigrettes, Camembert foams and hazelnut tempura) in his beautifully crafted dishes. Reserve ahead.

SaQuaNa
GASTRONOMY €€€

(☑ 02 31 89 40 80; 22 place Hamelin; menus from €100; ⊙ 12.30-2.30pm & 7.30-9.30pm Thu-Sat) This celebrated two-Michelin-starred restaurant dazzles with its exquisite, brilliantly inventive dishes. Chef Alexandre Bourdas trained in Japan (*sakana* means fish in Japanese, but also plays on French artistry in the realm of '*SAveur* (flavour), *QUalité* (quality) and *NAture*'), and he brings elements of the Far East to incredibly fresh, locally sourced ingredients.

❶ Information

Tourist Office (☑ 02 31 89 23 30; www.ot-honfleur.fr; quai Lepaulmier; ⊙ 9.30am-12.30pm & 2-6pm Mon-Sat Sep-Jun, 9.30am-7pm Jul & Aug, also 10am-5pm Sun Easter-Sep; 🛜)

Lille, Flanders & the Somme

With its dramatic land and sea views, deeply rooted culture, culinary traditions that include freshly caught seafood, age-old Flemish recipes and locally brewed beers, Hauts-de-France (Upper France) competes with the best the country has to offer.

History

In the Middle Ages, the Nord *département* (the sliver of France along the Belgian border), together with much of Belgium and part of the Netherlands, belonged to a feudal principality known as Flanders (Flandre or Flandres in French, Vlaanderen in Dutch). French Flanders takes in the areas of French Westhoek (around Dunkirk) and Walloon Flanders (around Lille).

Today, many people in the French Westhoek area still speak French Flemish (French Flemish: *Fransch vlaemsch;* French: *flamand français;* Dutch: *Frans-Vlaams*), a regional language that closely resembles West Flemish, though it differs to standard Dutch, which was based on northern Netherlands dialects. In Walloon Flanders, the traditional language is *picard,* also known as *ch'ti, chtimi* or *rouchi.*

The area south of the Somme estuary and Albert, Picardy (Picardie), historically centred on the Somme *département,* which saw some of the bloodiest fighting of WWI. The popular British WWI love song 'Roses of Picardy' was penned here in 1916 by Frederick E Weatherley.

In 2016, the former *régions* of Nord-Pas-de-Calais and Picardie merged, becoming the *région* of Hauts-de-France.

LILLE

POP 233.900

Capital of the Hauts-de-France *région,* Lille may be France's most underrated metropolis. Recent decades have seen the country's fourth-largest city (by greater urban area) transform from an industrial centre into a glittering cultural and commercial hub. Highlights include its enchanting old town with magnificent French and Flemish architecture, renowned art museums, stylish shopping, outstanding cuisine, a nightlife scene bolstered by 67,000 university students, and some 1600 designers in its environs.

In 2020, Lille will become the World Design Capital (the first French city to do so), with design agencies and other creative enterprises opening their doors to the public, and exhibitions and festivities throughout the year.

Thanks to the Eurostar and the TGV, Lille makes an easy, environmentally sustainable weekend destination from London, Paris, Brussels and beyond.

◉ Sights & Activities

★ **Palais des Beaux Arts**   MUSEUM
(Fine Arts Museum; ☏ 03 20 06 78 00; www.pba-lille.fr; place de la République; adult/child

€7/4; ⊙2-6pm Mon, 10am-6pm Wed-Sun; Ⓜ République-Beaux-Arts) Inaugurated in 1892, Lille's illustrious Fine Arts Museum claims France's second-largest collection after Paris' Musée du Louvre. Its cache of sublime 15th- to 20th-century paintings include works by Rubens, Van Dyck and Manet. Exquisite porcelain and *faïence* (pottery), much of it of local provenance, is on the ground floor, while in the basement you'll find classical archaeology, medieval statuary and 18th-century scale models of the fortified cities of northern France and Belgium.

Musée d'Art Moderne, d'Art Contemporain et d'Art Brut – LaM MUSEUM

(☑ 03 20 19 68 68; www.musee-lam.fr; 1 allée du Musée, Villeneuve-d'Ascq; adult/child €7/5, 1st Sun of month free; ⊙ museum 10am-6pm Tue-Sun, sculpture park 9am-6pm Tue-Sun) Colourful, playful and just plain weird works of modern and contemporary art by masters such as Braque, Calder, Léger, Miró, Modigliani and Picasso are the big draw at this renowned museum and sculpture park in the Lille suburb of Villeneuve-d'Ascq, 9km east of Gare Lille-Europe. Take metro line 1 to Pont de Bois, then bus L4 six stops to 'LaM'.

★ La Piscine Musée d'Art et d'Industrie GALLERY

(☑ 03 20 69 23 60; www.roubaix-lapiscine.com; 23 rue de l'Espérance, Roubaix; ⊙ 11am-6pm Tue-Thu, to 8pm Fri, 1-6pm Sat & Sun; Ⓜ Gare Jean Lebas)

An art deco municipal swimming pool built between 1927 and 1932 is now an innovative museum showcasing fine arts (paintings, sculptures, drawings) and applied arts (furniture, textiles, fashion) in a delightfully watery environment: the pool is still filled and sculptures are reflected in the water. Reopened in October 2018 with a new wing and 2000 sq metres of additional exhibition space; check the website for updated entry prices. It's 12km northeast of Gare Lille-Europe in Roubaix.

Hôtel de Ville HISTORIC BUILDING

(☑ 03 20 49 50 00; www.lille.fr; place Augustin Laurent CS; belfry adult/child €7/5.50; ⊙ belfry 10am-1pm & 2-5.30pm; Ⓜ Mairie de Lille) Built between 1924 and 1932, Lille's city hall is topped by a slender, 104m-high belfry that was designated a Unesco-listed monument

MEI QIANBAO/SHUTTERSTOCK ©

Lille

Lille

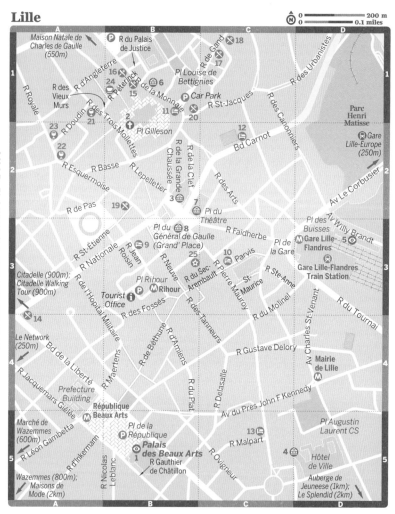

N 0 ———————— 200 m
   0 ———————— 0.1 miles

in 2004. Climbing 100 steps leads to a lift that whisks you to the top for a stunning panorama over the town. An audioguide costs €2; binoculars are available for €1. Ring the doorbell to gain entry.

Wazemmes   AREA
(M Gambetta) For an authentic taste of grassroots Lille, head to the ethnically diverse, family-friendly *quartier populaire* (working-class quarter) of Wazemmes, 1.3km southwest of place du Général de Gaulle, where old-school proletarians and immigrants live harmoniously alongside students and trendy *bobos* (bourgeois bohemians).

The neighbourhood's focal point is the cavernous **Marché de Wazemmes** (www. halles-wazemmes.com; place de la Nouvelle Aventure; ⊙ covered market 8am-8pm Tue-Sat, to 3pm Sun, street market 7am-2pm Tue, Thu & Sun; M Gambetta), Lille's favourite food market. The adjacent outdoor market is the place to be on Sunday morning – it's a real carnival scene. Rue des Sarrazins and rue Jules Guesde are lined with shops, restaurants and Tunisian bakeries, many owned by,

Lille

and catering to, the area's North African residents.

Wazemmes is famed for its outdoor concerts and street festivals, including La Louche d'Or (The Golden Ladle; 1 May), a soup festival that has spread to cities across Europe.

**Maison Natale de
Charles de Gaulle**   MUSEUM
(☑ 03 59 73 00 30; www.charles-de-gaulle.org; 9 rue Princesse; adult/child incl audioguide €6/free; ☉ 10am-noon & 2-5pm Wed-Sat, 1.30-5pm Sun; ⓜ Rihour) The upper-middle-class house in which Charles de Gaulle was born in 1890 is now a museum presenting the French general and president in the context of his times, with an emphasis on his connection to French Flanders. Displays include de Gaulle's baptismal robe and some evocative newsreels.

Musée de l'Hospice Comtesse   GALLERY
(☑ 03 28 36 84 00; www.lille.fr; 32 rue de la Monnaie; adult/child €3.60/free, audioguide €2; ☉ 2-6pm Mon, 10am-6pm Wed-Sun; ⓜ Rihour) Within a red-brick 15th- and 17th-century poorhouse, this absorbing museum features ceramics, earthenware wall tiles, religious art, 17th- and 18th-century paintings and furniture, and a detailed exhibit on the history of Lille. A rood screen separates the Salle des Malades (Hospital Hall), host-

ing contemporary art exhibitions, from a mid-17th-century chapel (look up to see a mid-19th-century painted ceiling).

Le Tripostal   ARTS CENTRE
(☑ 03 20 14 47 60; www.facebook.com/letripo; av Willy Brandt; prices vary; ☉ 10am-7pm Wed-Sat, hours can vary; ⓜ Gare Lille-Flandres) Splashed with street art murals, this cavernous red-brick postal sorting centre was transformed into an arts centre in 2004, when Lille was the European Capital of Culture. Changing art and photography exhibitions (most free) usually feature local artists; there's also a bar, canteen-style restaurant, a kids' play area and a design shop. Look out too for events such as DJ sets, live music gigs and workshops.

Citadelle   FORTRESS
(https://citadellelille.fr; av du 43e Régiment d'Infanterie; ☐ 10) At the northwestern end of bd de la Liberté, this massive, star-shaped fortress was designed by renowned 17th-century French military architect Vauban after France captured Lille in 1667, and completed in 1670. Made of some 60 million bricks, it now serves as the headquarters of the 12-nation, NATO-certified Rapid Reaction Corps – France. The only way to visit is by **guided tour** (☑ 03 59 57 94 00; www.lilletourism.com; av du 43e Régiment d'Infanterie; €7.50;

Dancing in the Vieille Bourse (p42), Lille

⊘ 3pm & 4.30pm Sun Jun-Aug, 3rd Sun of month Sep-May; 🚊 10).

Outside the 2.2km-long ramparts is central Lille's largest public park, the Parc de la Citadelle, spanning 60 hectares.

🎊 Festivals & Events

Braderie de Lille MARKET
(www.braderie-de-lille.fr; ⊘ early Sep) On the first weekend in September, Lille's entire city centre – 200km of footpaths – is transformed into what's billed as the world's largest flea market. It runs nonstop – yes, all night long – from 2pm on Saturday to 11pm on Sunday, when street sweepers emerge to tackle the mounds of mussel shells and old *frites* (fries) left behind by the merrymakers.

Marché de Noël CHRISTMAS MARKET
(www.noel-a-lille.com; place Rihour; ⊘ mid-Nov–late Dec) The neoclassical and Flemish buildings of place Rihour provide a magical backdrop for one of France's most enchanting Christmas markets. In the lead-up to Christmas, some 90 wooden stalls sell decorations, spiced biscuits, mulled wine and other seasonal treats; a funfair also sets up here.

🛏 Sleeping

Auberge de Jeunesse HOSTEL €
(📞 03 20 57 08 94; www.hifrance.org; 235 bd Paul Painlevé; dm incl breakfast & sheets €25; @ 🛜; Ⓜ Porte de Valenciennes) With a façade sporting the colours of Europe, Lille's youth hostel opened in 2015. The 55 spartan rooms have metal bunks, lockers and showers (with timer buttons), but only 12 have attached toilets. There's bike storage, a laundry and a self-catering kitchen. Wi-fi is available only in the lobby. It's 1.7km southeast of Gare Lille-Flandres.

★**Hôtel L'Arbre Voyageur** DESIGN HOTEL €€
(📞 03 20 20 62 62; http://hotelarbrevoyageur. com; 45 bd Carnot; d/f/ste from €119/214/219; ❄ 🛜; Ⓜ Gare Lille-Flandres) 🌿 Behind a fretted glass-and-steel façade in the former Polish Consulate's post-Soviet building, the 2016-opened Hôtel L'Arbre Voyageur has 48 stylised rooms (including four suites) with custom-made furniture and mini-bars stocked with free soft drinks, and a bamboo- and palm-filled courtyard. Green initiatives span solar panels to a free drink for guests who don't want their linen changed every day.

Grand Hôtel Bellevue HISTORIC HOTEL €€
(📞 03 20 57 45 64; www.grandhotelbellevue.com; 5 rue Jean Roisin; d from €138, with city views from €219; ❄ @ 🛜; Ⓜ Rihour) Opened in 1913, this venerable establishment has 60 spacious rooms with high ceilings, all-marble bathrooms, gilded picture frames and a mix of inlaid-wood antiques and ultramodern furnishings. Higher-priced rooms have sweep-

ing views of place du Général de Gaulle. A lavish buffet is laid on at breakfast (€16).

Hôtel de la Treille
HOTEL €€

(☏03 20 55 45 46; www.hoteldelatreille.com; 7-9 place Louise de Bettignies; s/d from €93/109; 🖥; Ⓜ Gare Lille-Flandres) In a superb spot smack in the middle of Vieux Lille, a few steps from dining and shopping options galore, Hôtel de la Treille's 42 stylish rooms offer views of the lively square out front, the cathedral or a quiet interior courtyard.

Hôtel Brueghel
HOTEL €€

(☏03 20 06 06 69; www.hotel-brueghel-lille. com; 5 parvis St-Maurice; s/d/apt from €79/90/250; 🖥; Ⓜ Gare Lille-Flandres) Hôtel Brueghel's 1930s-styled wood-panelled lobby has charm in spades, as does the tiny, old-fashioned lift that trundles guests up to 61 quiet rooms with modern furnishings and art posters on the walls. Some south-facing rooms have sunny views of the adjacent church. It also rents two city-centre apartments.

★ L'Hermitage Gantois
HOTEL €€€

(☏03 20 85 30 30; www.hotelhermitagegantois. com; 224 rue Pierre Mauroy; d/ste from €169/442; 🅿 @ 🖥 ≋; Ⓜ Mairie de Lille) This five-star hotel creates enchanting, harmonious spaces by complementing its rich architectural heritage, such as the Flemish-Gothic façade, with refined ultramodernism. The 89 rooms are sumptuous, with Philippe Starck accessories alongside Louis XV–style chairs and bathrooms that sparkle with Carrara marble. The still-consecrated chapel dates from 1637; there's a 12m pool and *hammam* (Turkish steambath).

✕ Eating

The dining scene in Lille is flourishing. You'll find Flemish specialities at *estaminets* (traditional Flemish eateries, with antique knick-knacks on the walls and plain wooden tables). Moderately priced French and Flemish restaurants line rue de Gand, while the area including rue de la Monnaie and its surrounding side streets is also a good bet.

★ Meert
PASTRIES €

(☏03 20 57 07 44; www.meert.fr; 27 rue Esquermoise; waffles & pastries €3-7.60, tearoom dishes €4.50-11.50, restaurant mains €26-32; ⏰ shop 2-7.30pm Mon, 9.30am-7.30pm Tue-Fri, 9am-7.30pm Sat, 9am-7pm Sun, tearoom 2-7pm Mon, 9.30am-10pm Tue-Fri, 9am-10pm Sat, 9am-6.30pm Sun, res-

taurant noon-2.30pm & 7.30-10pm Tue-Sat, 11am-2pm Sun; 🖥; Ⓜ Rihour) Famed for its *gaufres* (waffles) made with Madagascar vanilla, Meert has served kings, viceroys and generals since 1761. The sumptuous chocolate shop's coffered ceiling, painted wooden panels, wrought-iron balcony and mosaic floor date from 1839. Its *salon de thé* (tearoom) is a delightful spot for a morning Arabica or a mid-afternoon tea. Also here is a French gourmet restaurant.

Papà Raffaele
PIZZA €

(www.facebook.com/paparaffaelepizzeria; 5 rue St-Jacques; pizza €7.50-14; ⏰ noon-2pm & 7-10pm Mon-Thu, noon-2pm & 6.30-11pm Fri, noon-3pm & 6.30-11pm Sat & Sun; 🖋 🍴; Ⓜ Gare Lille-Flandres) The queues at Papà Raffaele are as legendary as its pizzas (it doesn't take reservations), so come early or late to this post-industrial space with recycled timber tables, vintage chairs and cured meats hanging from the ceiling. Wood-fired pizzas (like Cheesus Christ, with six cheeses) are made with Naples-sourced ingredients; coffee, craft beers and wine are all Italian. Takeaway is available.

La Clairière
VEGAN €

(☏03 20 11 23 16; www.facebook.com/LaClairiere-Lille; 75 bd de la Liberté; 2-/3-course midweek lunch menus €14/18, 2-/3-course dinner menus €16/20, mains €11-12, Sun brunch €22; ⏰ noon-2.30pm Tue-Thu, noon-2.30pm & 7.30-10pm Fri & Sat,

---

SHOP TALK

The snazziest fashion and homewares boutiques are in Vieux Lille, in the area bounded by rue de la Monnaie, rue Esquermoise, rue de la Grande Chausée and rue d'Angleterre. Design shops concentrate on rue du Faubourg des Poste, 3km southwest of the centre.

Keep an eye out for gourmet shops with locally made specialities such as chocolate. At **Maison Benoit** (☏03 20 31 69 03; https://maison-benoit. com; 77 rue de la Monnaie; ⏰10am-7pm Mon-Sat, 9.30am-1pm Sun; Ⓜ Rihour), second-generation artisan chocolatier Dominique Benoit creates pralines and other chocolates using traditional techniques and inspired flavour pairings, such as Cointreau and caramel, Bavarian vanilla and cherries, Périgord walnuts and chicory.

noon-2pm Sun; 🛜🍴♿; Ⓜ Rihour, République–Beaux Arts) In a bare-timber space with mezzanine seating, La Clairière creates colourful, 100% organic vegan cuisine made from sustainable produce (no palm oil). Most is locally sourced, including herbs and flowers grown in its planter boxes on the pavement out front. Menu highlights include roast butternut pumpkin stuffed with chestnuts, soy beans and carrots, and a squash, quinoa and mushroom crumble.

Le Bistrot Lillois
FRENCH, FLEMISH €

(☑ 03 20 14 04 15; 40 rue de Gand; mains €13-24; ⊙ noon-2pm & 7.30-10pm Tue-Sat; Ⓜ Rihour) Dishes both Flemish and French are served here under hanging hops. The highlight of the menu is *os à moëlle* (bone marrow); Flemish dishes worth trying include *carbonade flamande* (braised beef slow-cooked with beer, onions, brown sugar and gingerbread) and *potjevleesch* (jellied chicken, pork, veal and rabbit; served cold). Book ahead for dinner, or try arriving promptly at 7.30pm.

★ L'Assiette du Marché
FRENCH €€

(☑ 03 20 06 83 61; www.assiettedumarche.com; 61 rue de la Monnaie; 2-/3-course menus €19.50/25, mains €16-25; ⊙ noon-2.30pm & 7-10.30pm Mon-Fri, to 11pm Sat & Sun; Ⓜ Rihour) Entered via a grand archway, a 12th-century aristocratic mansion – a mint under Louis XIV, hence the street's name, and a listed historical monument – is the romantic setting for contemporary cuisine (tuna carpaccio with Champagne vinaigrette, roast duckling with glazed turnips and smoked garlic). Dine under its glass roof, in its intimate dining rooms, or on its cobbled courtyard in summer.

Le Barbier qui Fume
BARBECUE €€

(☑ 03 20 06 99 35; www.lebarbierquifume.fr; 69 rue de la Monnaie; 3-course lunch/dinner menu €17.40/28, mains €15-29.50; ⊙ 10.30am-3pm & 6-11pm Mon-Fri, 10.30am-11pm Sat, 11am-4pm Sun; Ⓜ Rihour) Charred aromas waft from this former barber shop (hence the name, the Smoking Barber), which now houses a ground-floor butcher and upstairs restaurant specialising in premium meats (pork knuckle, lamb shoulder, beef ribs) and poultry (pigeon, duck) smoked onsite over beechwood. There's a handful of tables next to the butcher's counter, and more out on the terrace.

Le Clair de Lune
FRENCH €€

(☑ 03 20 51 46 55; www.restaurant-leclairdelune.fr; 50 rue de Gand; 2-/3-course midweek lunch menus €16/20, dinner menus €28/36, mains €20; ⊙ noon-2pm & 7-10pm Mon, Tue & Thu, noon-2pm & 7-10.30pm Fri, noon-2.30pm & 7-10.30pm Sat, 12.30-2.30pm & 7-10pm Sun; Ⓜ Rihour) Creations such as duck carpaccio with gingerbread vinaigrette, beef fillet with red wine and chocolate jus, and guinea fowl with smoked bacon *crème* have seen Sébastien Defrance's elegant restaurant awarded the prestigious title Maître Restaurateur, a French government recognition of quality local produce and homemade cooking, in 2017. Around half of the 50-strong wine list is available by the glass.

🍷 Drinking & Nightlife

Lille is a bastion of the area's long-standing tradition of beer brewing; look out for beers from the region around town. Small, stylish bars line rue Royale and rue de la Barre, while university students descend on the bars along rue Masséna and rue Solférino, as far southeast as Marché Sébastopol. In warm weather, cafes on place du Général de Gaulle and place du Théâtre spill onto table-filled terraces.

Tamper
COFFEE

(☑ 03 20 39 28 21; 10 rue des Vieux Murs; ⊙ 9am-6pm Wed-Sat, to 5pm Sun; 🛜; Ⓜ Rihour) Beans roasted by Berlin's The Barn are brewed using filter, Aeropress, siphon or piston methods at this hip cafe with bare-brick walls and vintage American jazz on the turntable. It also serves iced teas and coffee, fresh OJ, homemade lemonade and smoothies, along with pastries and cakes.

Granola, eggs and French toast are among the options at breakfast; at lunch there are quiches, *tartines* (open sandwiches), salads and soups.

★ La Capsule
CRAFT BEER

(☑ 03 20 42 14 75; www.bar-la-capsule.fr; 25 rue des Trois Mollettes; ⊙ 5.30pm-1am Mon-Wed, 5.30pm-3am Thu & Fri, 4pm-3am Sat, 5.30pm-midnight Sun; 🛜; Ⓜ Rihour) Spread across three levels – a vaulted stone cellar, beamed-ceilinged ground floor and an upper level reached by a spiral staircase – Lille's best craft beer bar has 28 varieties on tap and over 100 by the bottle. Most are French (such as Lille's Lydéric and Paris' BapBap)

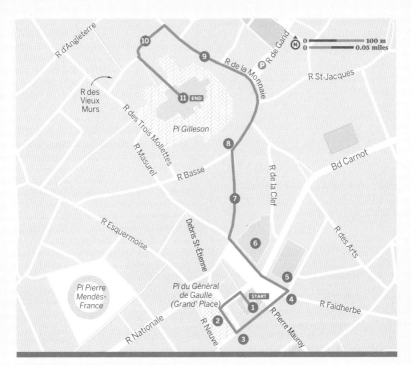

Walking Tour
Lille Discovery Stroll

START PLACE DU GÉNÉRAL DE GAULLE
END CATHÉDRALE NOTRE-DAME-DE-LA-TREILLE
LENGTH 1KM; ONE HOUR

The best place to begin a discovery stroll through Lille's Flemish heart is the city's focal point, **1 place du Général de Gaulle** (the Grand' Place), where you can admire the 1932 art deco home of **2 La Voix du Nord** (the leading regional newspaper), crowned by a gilded sculpture of the Three Graces. The goddess-topped victory column (1845) in the fountain commemorates the city's successful resistance to the Austrian siege of 1792. On warm evenings, Lillois come here to stroll, take in the urban vibe and sip a strong local beer.

The adjacent **3 Vieille Bourse** (p42; the old stock exchange) is ornately decorated with caryatids and cornucopia, a Flemish Renaissance extravaganza. Built in 1653, it consists of 24 separate houses set around a richly ornamented courtyard that hosts a used-book market. In the afternoon, especially on weekends, locals gather here to play *échecs* (chess).

Just east of the Vieille Bourse, impressive **4 place du Théâtre** is dominated by the Louis XVI–style **5 Opéra** (p88) and the neo-Flemish **6 Chambre de Commerce**, topped by a 76m-high spire sporting a gilded clock.

Vieux Lille (Old Lille), filled with restored 17th- and 18th-century brick houses, begins just north of here. It's hard to believe today, but in the late 1970s much of this quarter was a half-abandoned slum dominated by empty, dilapidated buildings. Head north past the outdoor cafes to **7 rue de la Grande Chaussée**, lined with Lille's chicest shops. Continue north along **8 rue de la Monnaie** (named after a mint constructed here in 1685), whose old brick residences now house boutiques and the **9 Musée de l'Hospice Comtesse** (p83).

Turning left (west) on tiny **10 rue Péter-inck** and then left again will take you to the 19th-century, neogothic **11 Cathédrale Notre-Dame-de-la-Treille**, which has a strikingly modern west façade that looks better from inside or when illuminated at night.

and Belgian (eg Cantillon), but small-scale brewers from around the world are also represented.

L'Illustration Café
BAR

(☑ 03 20 12 00 90; 18 rue Royale; ⊘noon-1am Mon & Tue, 12.30pm-1am Wed, noon-3am Thu & Fri, 2.30pm-3am Sat, 3pm-1am Sun; Ⓜ Rihour) Adorned with art nouveau woodwork and changing exhibits by local painters, this laid-back bar attracts artists, musicians, budding intellectuals and teachers in the mood to read, exchange weighty ideas or just shoot the breeze. The mellow soundtrack mixes jazz, blues, indie rock, French *chansons* and African and Cuban beats. Check the Facebook page for details of concerts.

Le Privilège
GAY

(www.facebook.com/privilege.lille; 2 rue Royale; ⊘5pm-1am Sun-Wed, 5pm-3am Thu & Fri, 3pm-3am Sat; 🖥; Ⓜ Rihour) In a former bookshop, Lille's premier gay bar has a vaulted cellar, ground-floor bar/dance floor strung with mirrored disco balls, and an upper-level bar. Most nights see DJs spinning disco, pop and electronica. Tuesdays is retro ('80s and '90s tunes); on Wednesdays it hosts drag karaoke.

Le Network
CLUB

(☑ 03 20 40 04 91; www.lenetwork.fr; 15 rue du Faisan; ⊘10.30pm-7am Tue, Wed, Fri & Sat, 9.30pm-7am Thu, 7pm-7am Sun; Ⓜ République–Beaux Arts) Central Lille's hottest club has two dance floors, three bars, plenty of flashing lights and space for 700 revellers. On most nights the music is three-quarters house and electronic and a quarter R&B. Dress up as the door policy is pretty strict. Admission ranges from free to €15 (including a drink), depending on what's happening.

☆ Entertainment

Lille's free French-language entertainment guide *Sortir* (http://hautsdefrance.sortir. eu), issued every Wednesday, is available at the tourist office, cinemas, event venues and bookshops. For arts exhibitions and events, check www.lille3000.com.

Lille's Opéra (☑ tickets 08 20 48 90 00; www. opera-lille.fr; place du Théâtre; Ⓜ Rihour) hosts opera, dance and classical concerts.

Buy entertainment tickets at Fnac (www. fnacspectacles.com; 20 rue St-Nicolas; ⊘10am-7.30pm Mon-Sat; Ⓜ Rihour).

Le Splendid
LIVE MUSIC

(☑ 03 20 33 20 17; www.le-splendid.com; 1 place du Mont de Terre; Ⓜ Porte de Valenciennes) A former cinema with balcony seating is now one of Lille's best live music venues, with a capacity of 900. Local and international rock, indie and pop acts all play here; there are around 70 to 100 concerts per year.

ⓘ Information

Tourist Office (☑ 03 59 57 94 00; www. lilletourism.com; 3 rue du Palais Rihour;

THE GIANTS

In far northern France and nearby Belgium, *géants* (giants) – wickerwork body masks up to 8.5m tall animated by someone (or several someones) inside – emerge for local carnivals and on feast days to dance and add to the general merriment. Each has a name and a personality, usually based on the Bible, legends or local history. Giants are born, baptised, grow up, marry and have children, creating, over the years, complicated family relationships. They serve as important symbols of town, neighbourhood and village identity.

Medieval in origin – and also found in places such as the UK, Catalonia, the Austrian Tyrol, Mexico, Brazil and India – giants have been a tradition in northern France since the 16th century. More than 300 of the creatures now 'live' in French towns, including Arras, Boulogne, Calais, Cassel, Dunkirk and Lille. France and Belgium's giants were recognised by Unesco as 'masterpieces of the oral and intangible heritage of humanity' in 2005.

Your best chance to see them is at pre-Lenten carnivals, during Easter and at festivals held from May to September, often on weekends. Dates and places appear in the free, annual poster-brochure *C'est quand les géants?*, available at tourist offices and online at www.calendrier-des-geants.eu.

Place des Héros, Arras

9.30am-1pm & 2-6pm Mon-Sat, 10am-12.30pm & 1.15-4.30pm Sun; Ⓜ Rihour)

❶ Getting Around

BICYCLE

Operated by Transpole, Lille's bike-sharing scheme **V-Lille** (www.transpole.fr; day/week subscription €1.60/7, 1st 30min free, every subsequent 30min €1; ⊘ 24hr) has 2200 bikes at stations across town.

PUBLIC TRANSPORT

Lille's two speedy metro lines (1 and 2), two tramways (R and T), two Citadine shuttles (C1, which circles the city centre clockwise, and C2, which goes counterclockwise) and many urban and suburban bus lines – several of which cross into Belgium – are run by Transpole (www.transpole.fr).

Tickets (€1.60, plus €0.20 for a reusable ticket) can be bought on buses, but must be purchased before boarding a metro or tram from one of the ticket machines at each stop. A Pass' Journée (24-hour pass) costs €4.80 and must be time-stamped each time you board; two- to seven-day passes are also available. A Pass Soirée, good for unlimited travel after 7pm, costs €2.20.

There is a Transpole **ticket office** (🖉 03 20 40 40 40; www.transpole.fr; Gare Lille-Flandres; ⊘ 6.30am-8pm Mon-Fri, 9am-8pm Sat; Ⓜ Gare Lille-Flandres) adjacent to the Gare Lille-Flandres metro station.

FLANDERS & ARTOIS

Arras

POP 40,720

An unexpected gem of a city, Artois' former capital Arras (the final 's' is pronounced) has an exceptional ensemble of Flemish-style arcaded buildings – the main squares are especially lovely at night – and two subterranean WWI sites. The city makes a good base for visits to the Battle of the Somme memorials.

◉ Sights & Activities

★ **Grand' Place &**
Place des Héros   SQUARE

Arras' two ancient market squares, the Grand' Place and the almost-adjacent, smaller place des Héros (also known as the Petite Place), are surrounded by 17th- and 18th-century Flemish Baroque houses topped by curvaceous gables. Although the structures vary in decorative detail, their 345 sandstone columns form a common arcade unique in France. Like 80% of Arras, both squares – especially handsome at night – were heavily damaged during WWI, so many of the gorgeous façades were reconstructed after the war.

Hôtel de Ville · · · · · · · · · · · · · · · · HISTORIC BUILDING

(☑ 03 21 51 26 95; place des Héros; city hall tours adult/child €4.20/3, belfry adult/child €3.10/2.10, boves tour €5.40/3.20; ⊙ 9am-6.30pm Mon-Sat, 10am-1pm & 2.30-6.30pm Sun early Apr–mid-Sep, shorter hours mid-Sep–early Apr, boves closed Jan) Arras' Flemish Gothic city hall dates from the 16th century but was completely rebuilt after WWI. Four *géants* (giants) live in the lobby. For a panoramic view, take the lift (plus 43 stairs) up the 75m-high, Unesco-listed belfry. Or, for a subterranean perspective, head down into the *souterrains* (caves) under the square, also known as *boves,* which were turned into British command posts, hospitals and barracks during WWI.

Tours of the *boves* (40 minutes; in English upon request) generally begin at 11am, with at least two more departures in the afternoon. City hall tours run at 3pm Sunday year-round, with an additional tour at 3pm Monday to Friday July and August. Tickets are sold at the tourist office (on the ground floor).

Carrière Wellington · · · · · · · · · · · · · · · · HISTORIC SITE

(p44)

🛏 Sleeping

Place du Maréchal Foch, in front of the train station, has a number of midrange hotels.

★ **La Corne d'Or** · · · · · · · · · · · · · · · · B&B €€

(☑ 03 21 58 85 94; www.lamaisondhotes.com; 1 place Guy Mollet; s/d/ste/loft incl breakfast from €110/125/140/145; 🛜) Occupying a magnificent *hôtel particulier* (private mansion) built in 1748, this romantic B&B is filled with antiques, art and books on WWI. Some of the five imaginatively designed rooms and suites still have their original woodwork, gilded mirrors, marble fireplaces and stained glass. Australian host Rodney, formerly of Australia's Department of Veterans' Affairs, is a great resource.

Hôtel Les 3 Luppars · · · · · · · · · · · · · · · · HOTEL €€

(☑ 03 21 60 02 03; www.hotel-les3luppars.com; 49 Grand' Place; s/d/tr/q from €88/105/115/125; @🛜) Occupying the Grand' Place's only non-Flemish-style building (it's Gothic and dates from the 1400s), Les 3 Luppars (derived from 'Leopards') has a private courtyard and 42 rooms, 10 with fine views of the square. The decor is uninspired, but the location is great and the atmosphere is welcoming. Amenities include a sauna (€6 per person).

Grand Place Hôtel · · · · · · · · · · · · · · · · DESIGN HOTEL €€

(☑ 03 91 19 19 79; http://grandplacehotel.fr; 23 Grand' Place; d/ste/apt/loft from €102/120/150/170; ✳🛜) Behind one of the Grand' Place's few Flemish Baroque façades to escape wartime damage, this 2015-opened hotel has a dozen rooms done out in stylish black and white. Some suites and the apartments sleep four, while the loft sleeps six; apartments and the loft also come with kitchenettes.

🍴 Eating

Lots of restaurants are tucked away under the arches of the Grand' Place, place des Héros and – connecting the two – rue de la Taillerie.

Marché à Arras · · · · · · · · · · · · · · · · MARKET €

(place des Héros, Grand' Place & place de la Vacquerie; ⊙ 8am-1pm Wed & Sat) Arras' twice-weekly food market stretches across the city's three central squares; Saturday's market is especially huge.

Le Petit Rat Porteur · · · · · · · · · · · · · · · · BRASSERIE €

(☑ 03 21 51 29 70; 11 rue de la Taillerie; mains €10-18.50; ⊙ noon-2pm & 7-9.30pm Tue-Sat, noon-2pm Sun) Beloved for its marvellous vaulted cellar and friendly staff, this buzzing brasserie has a great range of salads alongside regional standards including *potjevleesch* (aspic potted meat) and *waterzooi* (chicken stew).

Assiette au Bœuf · · · · · · · · · · · · · · · · GRILL €

(☑ 03 21 15 11 51; http://assietteauboeuf.fr; 56 Grand' Place; menus lunch €12-15.50, dinner €17-19.50; ⊙ noon-2.30pm & 7-11pm; 🖷) Hugely popular with locals for its great-value steaks, this Grand' Place restaurant also serves burgers and mixed grills.

La Faisanderie · · · · · · · · · · · · · · · · FRENCH €€

(☑ 03 74 11 64 69; www.restaurant-la-faisanderie.com; 45 Grand' Place; 3-course midweek lunch menu €25, 2-/3-course dinner menu €31/36, mains

€16-19; ⏱ 7-9.30pm Tue, noon-1.30pm & 7-9.30pm Wed-Sat, noon-1.30pm Sun) In a superb vaulted brick cellar, this formal restaurant serves a range of classical dishes prepared with carefully selected ingredients: oysters *naturelles,* Pernod-flambéed prawns, beef fillet with morel sauce or turbot with seared endives and beer sauce. The wine list is outstanding.

ℹ Information

Tourist Office (📞 03 21 51 26 95; www.explorearras.com; place des Héros; ⏱ 9am-6.30pm Mon-Sat, 10am-1pm & 2.30-6.30pm Sun early Apr–mid-Sep, shorter hours mid-Sep–early Apr; 🛈)

ℹ Getting Around

Arras is setting up a shared bicycle scheme; contact the tourist office for details.

SOMME BATTLEFIELDS MEMORIALS

The First Battle of the Somme, a WWI Allied offensive waged in the villages and woodlands northeast of Amiens, was designed to relieve pressure on the beleaguered French

troops at Verdun. On 1 July 1916, British, Commonwealth and French troops 'went over the top' in a massive assault along a 34km front. But German positions proved virtually unbreachable, and on the first day of the battle an astounding 19,240 British troops were killed and another 38,230 were wounded. Most casualties were infantrymen mown down by German machine guns. By the time the offensive was called off in mid-November, over one million men on both sides had been killed or wounded. The British had advanced 12km, the French 8km.

The Battle of the Somme has become a symbol of the meaningless slaughter of WWI, and its killing fields – along with those of the Battle of Arras and Western Front sectors further north – are now sites of pilgrimage. Each year, thousands of visitors from Australia, Canada, Great Britain, New Zealand, South Africa and other Commonwealth nations follow the Circuit du Souvenir (Remembrance Trail; www.somme-battlefields.com).

Convenient bases for exploring the area include Amiens, Arras and the small towns of Péronne, Albert and Pozières.

Somme Battlefields & Memorials

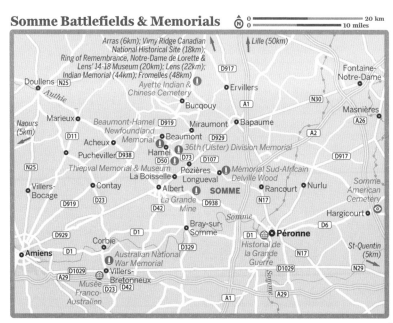

◉ Sights

Historial de la Grande Guerre   MUSEUM
(p47)

**Beaumont-Hamel
Newfoundland Memorial**   MEMORIAL
(☑ 03 22 76 70 86; www.veterans.gc.ca; rue de
l'Église, Beaumont-Hamel; ☻ visitor centre noon-
6pm Mon, 10am-6pm Tue-Sun Apr-Sep, 11am-
5pm Mon, 9am-5pm Tue-Sun Oct-Mar) `FREE`
This evocative memorial preserves part
of the Western Front in the state it was
in at fighting's end. The zigzag trench system, which still fills with mud in winter,
is clearly visible, as are countless shell
craters and the remains of barbed-wire
barriers. Canadian students based at
the Welcome Centre, which resembles a
Newfoundland fisher's house, give free
guided tours on the hour (except from
mid-December to mid-January). It's 9km
north of Albert; follow the signs for 'Memorial Terreneuvien'.

The memorial to the 29th Division, to
which the volunteer Royal Newfoundland
Regiment belonged, stands at the entrance
to the site. On 1 July 1916, this regiment
stormed entrenched German positions and
was nearly wiped out; until a few years
ago, a plaque noted bluntly that 'strategic
and tactical miscalculations led to a great
slaughter'. A path leads to an orientation table at the top of the Caribou mound, where
a bronze caribou statue is surrounded by
plants native to Newfoundland.

**Vimy Ridge Canadian
National Historic Site**   HISTORIC SITE, MEMORIAL
(p44)

**Fromelles (Pheasant Wood)
Cemetery & Museum**   CEMETERY, MUSEUM
(☑ 03 59 61 15 14; www.musee-bataille-fromelles.
fr; 2 rue de la Basse Ville, Fromelles; cemetery free,
museum adult/child €6.50/4; ☻ cemetery 24hr,
museum 9.30am-5.30pm Wed-Mon early Mar–mid-
Jan) On 19 July 1916, a poorly planned offensive using inexperienced Australian and
British troops was launched to divert German forces from the Battle of the Somme.
After the surviving Australians retreated
to their pre-battle front lines, hundreds of
their comrades-in-arms lay wounded in no
man's land. For three days the survivors
made heroic efforts to rescue them, acts
of bravery commemorated by the Cob-
bers sculpture in the Australian Memorial
Park, 2km northwest of the museum. Ross
McMullin, writing for the Australian War
Memorial (www.awm.gov.au), described the
battle as the worst 24 hours in Australia's
entire history.

It is likely that one of the soldiers on the
victorious German side was a 27-year-old
corporal in the 16th Bavarian Reserve Infantry Regiment named Adolf Hitler.

After the failed and catastrophic assault,
the Germans buried many of the Australian

Thiepval Memorial

SUBTERRANEAN DISCOVERY

Believed to date from the 3rd century AD, **La Cité Souterraine de Naours** (Caves of Naours; ☑ 03 22 93 71 78; http://citesouterrainedenaours.fr; 5 rue des Carrières, Naours; adult/child incl audioguide €11/7, incl 90min guided tour €12/9; ⊗ 10am-6.30pm Jul & Aug, 10am-5.30pm Tue-Fri, 10am-6.30pm Sat & Sun Apr-Jun, Sep & Oct, 11am-4.30pm Tue-Sun Feb, Mar & Nov) is an extraordinary underground 'city' of quarried tunnels. It was started by the Romans and expanded over the centuries, incorporating 28 galleries and 300 rooms, including three chapels, multiple town squares, a bakery (with working ovens) and livestock barns. Only rediscovered in 1887, it was used by Allied forces in WWI, and as a Nazi HQ in WWII. The temperature below ground is a constant 9.5°C; bring a jacket (and a torch/flashlight).

Soldiers' graffiti from both wars can be seen throughout the cave system. Guided tours are in English and French. The site is 18km north of Amiens.

and British dead in mass graves behind their lines. Most were reburied after the war, but five pits were not found for more than 90 years. DNA testing has established the identity of 144 Australians.

The 'Battle of Fromelles Walking Guide' has details on a 10km walking or driving tour of 10 WWI sites near Fromelles, which is 18km west of Lille.

Ring of Remembrance   MEMORIAL
(p43)

Lens' 14-18 Museum   MUSEUM
(☑ 03 21 74 83 15; www.lens14-18.com; 102 rue Pasteur, Souchez; audioguide €3; ⊗ 10am-1pm & 2-5pm Tue-Sun) **FREE** Housed in four black concrete cubes, this 2015-opened WWI museum provides an in-depth introduction to WWI on the Western Front. Over 300 extraordinary photos, carefully selected by historians from French, British and German archives, detail daily life and death in the trenches; also on display are some 60 hours of archival film. It's situated 2km west (down the hill) from the Ring of Remembrance (Notre-Dame de Lorette), on a hill overlooking Lens.

Musée Franco-Australien   MUSEUM
(Franco-Australian Museum; ☑ 03 22 96 80 79; www.museeaustralien.com; 9 rue Victoria, Villers-Bretonneux; adult/child €6/3; ⊗ 9.30am-5.30pm Apr-Oct, to 4.30pm Nov-late Dec & mid-Jan–Mar) Some 2400 Australian soldiers were killed or wounded in the April 1918 assault that wrested Villers-Bretonneux from German control. In the 1920s, Australian children donated funds to rebuild the town's primary school, creating bonds of friendship that remain strong to this day.

Part of Victoria School is now a museum featuring highly personal artefacts donated by Australian ex-servicemen and their families. It's located 20km east of Amiens via the D1029.

Somme American Cemetery   CEMETERY
(p47)

Thiepval Memorial & Museum   MEMORIAL, MUSEUM
(☑ 03 22 74 60 47; www.historial.org; rue de l'Ancre, Thiepval; memorial free, museum adult/child €6/3; ⊗ memorial 10am-5pm Tue-Sun Mar-Nov, 9.30am-6pm Mar-Oct, to 5pm Nov-early Dec & mid-Jan–Feb) Its silhouette instantly recognisable from afar, this 45m-high memorial to the missing of the Somme, 7.5km northeast of Albert, is inscribed with the names of more than 72,000 British and South African soldiers whose remains were never recovered or identified. Designed by Edwin Lutyens, it was built from 1928 to 1932 on the site of a German stronghold that was stormed on 1 July 1916, the bloody first day of the Battle of the Somme.

The museum, run by Péronne's outstanding Historial de la Grande Guerre (p47), opened in 2016; displays include uniforms and large installations such as a replica of French fighter ace Georges Guynemer's aeroplane. The visitor centre's bookshop has an excellent selection of English books on WWI.

Its adjacent joint French and Commonwealth cemetery expresses Franco-British fraternity in death as in life.

Ulster Memorial Tower   MEMORIAL
(☑ 03 22 74 81 11; www.somme14-18.com; rte de St-Pierre-Divion, Thiepval; ⊗ 10am-5pm Tue-Sun

Beaumont-Hamel Newfoundland Memorial (p92)
JON NICHOLLS PHOTOGRAPHY/SHUTTERSTOCK ©

Mar-Nov) FREE The 5000 Ulstermen who perished in the Battle of the Somme are commemorated by this 21m-high Gothic-style tower, an exact replica of Helen's Tower at Clanboye, County Down, where the Ulster Division trained. Dedicated in 1921, it has long been a Unionist pilgrimage site; a black obelisk known as the Orange Memorial to Fallen Brethren (1994) stands in an enclosure behind the tower. It's 1.2km northwest of Thiepval.

Virtually untouched since the war, nearby Thiepval Wood can be visited on a guided tour (donation requested); check the website for times and dates.

Neuve-Chapelle
Indian Memorial   MEMORIAL
(www.cwgc.org; 413 rue du Bois, Richebourg; ⊙24hr) FREE The Mémorial Indien, 27km southwest of Lille, records the names of 4700 soldiers and labourers of the Indian Army who 'have no known grave'. The 15m-high column, flanked by two tigers, is topped by a lotus capital, the British Crown and the Star of India. The units (31st Punjabis, 11th Rajputs, 2nd King Edward's Own Gurkha Rifles) and the ranks of the fallen – Sepoy (infantry private), Havildar (sergeant) – are engraved on the walls.

La Grande Mine   LANDMARK
(Lochnagar Crater Memorial; www.lochnagarcrater. org; rte de la Grande Mine, La Boisselle; ⊙24hr) FREE Just outside the hamlet of La Bois-

selle, 4.5km northeast of Albert, this enormous crater looks like the site of a meteor impact. Some 100m across and 30m deep, it was created on the morning of the first day of the First Battle of the Somme (1 July 1916) by 27 tonnes of ammonal (an explosive made from ammonium nitrate and aluminium powder) laid by British sappers in order to create a breach in the German front lines.

Mémorial Sud-Africain
Delville Wood   MEMORIAL, MUSEUM
(South African National Memorial & Museum; ☑03 22 85 02 17; www.delvillewood.com; rte de Ginchy, Longueval; ⊙memorial 24hr, museum 10am-5.30pm Apr–mid-Oct, to 4pm Feb, Mar & mid-Oct–Nov, closed Dec, Jan & South African public holidays) FREE The memorial (1926) and star-shaped museum (1986), a replica of Cape Town's Castle of Good Hope, stand in the middle of Delville Wood, where in July 1916 the 1st South African Infantry Brigade was nearly wiped out in hand-to-hand fighting that obliterated all the trees. In 2016, the names of all the South Africans who died in WWI were inscribed on a memorial wall.

During the 1916 offensive, pre-existing paths through Delville Wood were named for well-known streets in London and Edinburgh. Today, the area is still considered a cemetery because so many bodies were never recovered. Inside the museum, apartheid-era bronze murals portray black members of the South African Native Labour Corps (black South Africans were banned from combat roles) without shirts – despite the often chilly European weather. The memorial and museum are 15km east of Albert.

Ayette Indian & Chinese
Cemetery   CEMETERY
(www.cwgc.org; Vieux Chemin de Bucquoy, Ayette; ⊙24hr) FREE Towards the end of WWI, tens of thousands of Chinese labourers were recruited by the British government to perform noncombat jobs in Europe, including the gruesome task of recovering and burying Allied war dead. Some 80 of these *travailleurs chinois* (Chinese labourers) and Indians who served with British forces are buried in this Commonwealth cemetery, which is 15km south of Arras, just off the D919 at the southern edge of the village of Ayette.

Many Chinese labourers died in the Spanish flu epidemic of 1918–19. Their gravestones are etched in Chinese and English with inscriptions such as 'A good reputation endures forever', 'A noble duty bravely done' and 'Faithful unto death'. The nearby graves of Indians are marked in Hindi or Arabic.

Australian National War Memorial
MEMORIAL, MUSEUM

(https://sjmc.gov.au; rte de Villers-Bretonneux, Fouilloy; ☉memorial 24hr, museum 9.30am-6pm mid-Apr–Oct, to 5pm Nov–mid-Apr) **FREE** During WWI, 416,809 Australians – 8% of the country's population – volunteered for overseas military service; 46,000 met their deaths on the Western Front (14,000 others perished elsewhere). The names of 10,722 Australian soldiers whose remains were never found are engraved at the base of the Australian National War Memorial's 32m-high tower, which stands atop a gentle hill where Australian and British troops repulsed a German assault in April 1918. Behind the tower, the Sir John Monash Centre museum has interactive displays.

The viewing area atop the tower, damaged by German gunfire in 1940, affords panoramic views of a large Commonwealth cemetery with 779 Australian graves and the one-time battlefield. An Anzac Day Dawn Service is held here every 25 April at 5.30am. The memorial is 3km north of Villers-Bretonneux along the D23.

Fricourt German Cemetery
CEMETERY

(www.volksbund.de; 21 rue de Pozières, Fricourt; ☉24hr) **FREE** A stark reminder of the extensive loss of life on all sides of WWI, this cemetery is the burial place of 17,027 fallen German soldiers. Only 5000 of the graves are individual; the remainder of the dead lie in four mass graves. Many remains were interred from other cemeteries around the Somme in 1920.

🏃 Activities

Aero Dom
SCENIC FLIGHTS

(☑07 83 54 39 01; www.aero-dom.fr; rte de Paris, Roupy; 20/30/60min flight €80/100/175; ☉by reservation) If you have a head for heights, get a swooping aerial view over the Somme battlefields and memorials aboard a gyrocopter flight, where you sit behind the pilot in an open cockpit. Itineraries can be customised depending on your interests. Heated jackets and helmets will be provided. Flights depart 24km southeast of Péronne.

Amiens Balloon
BALLOONING

(☑06 07 68 74 44; www.amiensBALLOON.com; 7 rue du Laboureur, Sains-en-Amiénois; per person €220; ☉by reservation) Float over the Somme aboard a hot-air balloon, with commentary in English and French. Flight time is one hour but the whole experience lasts four hours; bring a jacket and wear flat shoes. Children under 1.2m tall (and expectant mothers) aren't permitted. The departure point is 11km south of Amiens; routes depend on wind direction.

👉 Tours

Tourist offices (including those in Amiens, Arras, Albert and Péronne) can help book tours of battlefield sites and memorials. Recommended tour companies include the following:

Battlefields Experience (☑03 22 76 29 60; www.thebattleofthesomme.co.uk; half-/full day per person incl museum entry fees €65/130)

Chemins d'Histoire (☑06 23 67 77 64; www.cheminsdhistoire.com; full day per person from €120)

Sacred Ground Tours (☑06 75 66 59 02; www.sacredgroundtours.com.au; full day per person from €200)

ℹ PICNIC PERFECT

Stock up on a picnic of local produce at the market before heading out for the day to the Somme battlefields and memorials.

Marché sur l'Eau (place Parmentier; ☉8am-1pm Sat) Fruit and veggies grown in Amiens' market gardens, the Hortillonnages, are sold at this one-time floating market, now held on dry land.

Halle au Frais (www.leshalles-amiens.fr; 22b rue du Général Leclerc; ☉9am-7pm Tue-Sat, to 12.30pm Sun) Two dozen stalls sell picnic supplies, including cheeses, breads and wine, at this covered market within Amiens' Les Halles shopping complex.

Terres de Mémoire (☑ 03 22 84 23 05; www.terresdememoire.com; full day per person from €130)

True Blue Digger Tours (☑ 06 01 33 46 76; http://trueblue-diggertours.com; half-day per person from €55)

Walkabout Digger Tours (☑ 06 64 54 16 63; http://walkaboutdiggertours.free.fr; full day per person from €120)

🛏 Sleeping & Eating

Amiens and Arras have a good range of accommodation options, but many visitors choose to stay in small hotels or B&Bs situated in towns closer to the battlefields, such as Péronne, Albert or Pozières. The latter towns all have ample restaurants and shops selling picnic supplies.

Au Vintage   B&B €

(☑ 03 22 75 63 28; www.chambres-dhotes-albert. com; 19 rue de Corbie, Albert; d incl breakfast €80-85; P 🛜) This delightful B&B, in a brick mansion from 1920, has two atmospheric rooms with old wooden floors, antique furnishings and marble fireplaces. Evelyne and Jacky are delightful, cultured hosts who enjoy sharing their knowledge about the battlefields with their guests; ask to see their three vintage cars. Reserve well ahead.

Butterworth Farm   B&B €

(☑ 03 22 75 26 46; www.butterworth-cottage. com; rte de Bazentin (D73), Pozières; s/d/q incl breakfast €65/80/110; P 🛜) Run by Bernard, the mayor of Pozières, and his wife, Marie, this well-kept B&B on their family farm has six individually decorated rooms with themes such as Out of Africa. Guests can unwind in the garden, which is filled with flowers and herbs; the copious breakfasts include quiche and freshly squeezed orange juice.

La Basilique   HOTEL €€

(☑ 03 22 75 04 71; www.hotelbasiliquesomme. fr; 3-5 rue Gambetta, Albert; d/tr from €92/102; 🛜) In the heart of Albert, right across the square from the basilica, this well-kept hotel has 10 neat rooms with French windows, bright bathrooms and richly patterned feature walls. The in-house restaurant (two-/three-course *menus* €18/22) specialises in *cuisine du terroir* (regional specialities made with quality local ingredients) such as duck breast with sour-cherry sauce. Breakfast costs €10.

Hôtel Le Saint-Claude   HOTEL €€

(☑ 03 22 79 49 49; www.hotelsaintclaude.com; 9 place du Commandant Louis Daudré, Péronne; s/d/tr from €76/93/125; 🛜) Originally a *relais de poste* (coaching inn), the Saint-Claude is located in the centre of Péronne just 200m from the medieval château housing the Historial de la Grande Guerre (p47). The hotel's 40 contemporary rooms are decorated in chic greys and creams and have ultramodern bathrooms; some have château views. The table-strewn walled courtyard is a suntrap.

ℹ Information

Albert Tourist Office (☑ 03 22 75 16 42; www.tourisme-paysducoquelicot.com; 9 rue Gambetta, Albert; ⊙ 9am-12.30pm & 1.30-6.30pm Mon-Fri, 9am-12.30pm & 2-6.30pm Sat, 9am-1pm Sun May-Aug, 9am-12.30pm & 1.30-5pm Mon-Fri, 9am-noon & 2-5pm Sat Sep-Apr)

Péronne Tourist Office (☑ 03 22 84 42 38; www.hautesomme-tourisme.com; 16 place André Audinot, Péronne; ⊙ 9.30am-12.30pm & 1.30-6.30pm Mon-Sat, 10am-noon & 2-5pm Sun Jul & Aug, 9am-12.30pm & 2-6pm Mon-Fri, 9am-noon & 2-6pm Sat Apr-Jun, Sep & Oct, shorter hour Nov-Mar)

ℹ Getting Around

You'll need your own transport (a car or bike) to visit most of the Somme battlefields and memorials. Bicycles can be rented at the tourist office in Albert (standard bike half-/full day €8/12, electric bike €15/25).

AMIENS

POP 133,450

Amiens' mostly pedestrianised city centre, tastefully rebuilt after WWII, is complemented by lovely green spaces along the Somme River. Jules Verne lived the last 34 years of his life here; his former home is now a museum. Some 30,000 students from the Université de Picardie Jules Verne give the town a youthful energy.

Amiens is an ideal base for visits to many of the Battle of the Somme memorials.

◉ Sights & Activities

Place Gambetta, the city's commercial hub, is three blocks southwest of the cathedral. Amiens' Quartier Anglais (English Quarter), 1.5km southeast of the train station, is a little piece of England built in the 1890s for the

Amiens

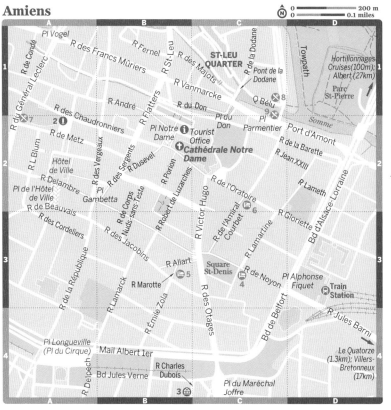

 amiens map with scale 0 200 m / 0 0.1 miles, N compass

Amiens

British managers of a textile factory (part of Sebastian Faulks' novel *Birdsong* is set here).

★**Cathédrale Notre Dame**　　　CATHEDRAL
(www.cathedrale-amiens.fr; 30 place Notre Dame; cathedral free, north tower adult/child €6/free, treasury €3.50/free, tower & treasury €8/free, audioguide €4; ⊘ cathedral 8.30am-5.15pm daily, north tower to mid-afternoon Wed-Mon) A Unesco World Heritage Site, the largest Gothic cathedral in France (at 145m long) and the

largest in the world by volume was begun in 1220 to house the skull of St John the Baptist. It's renowned for its soaring Gothic arches (42.3m high over the transept), unity of style and immense interior; look for the 17th-century statue known as the *Ange Pleureur* (Crying Angel), behind the Baroque high altar.

The octagonal, 234m-long labyrinth on the black-and-white floor of the nave is easy

97

Cathédrale Notre Dame (p97), Amiens

to miss as the soaring vaults draw the eye upward. Part of the skull of St John the Baptist, framed in gold and jewels, can be seen in the *trésor* (treasury). Plaques in the south transept honour American, Australian, British, Canadian and New Zealand soldiers who perished in WWI.

To get a sense of what you're seeing, it's worth hiring a multilingual audioguide at Amiens' tourist office. Weather permitting, visitors willing to brave 307 steps can climb the north tower for spectacular views; tickets are sold in the boutique to the left as you walk through the west façade. The cathedral is closed to visitors during religious ceremonies.

A free 45-minute light show bathes the cathedral's façade in vivid medieval colours nightly from mid-June to the third weekend in September, and from early December to 1 January. The photons start flying at 10.45pm in June, 10.30pm in July, 10pm in August, 9.45pm in September and 7pm in December.

Maison de Jules Verne   MUSEUM
(Maisons des Illustres; ☑ 03 22 45 45 75; www.amiens.fr; 2 rue Charles Dubois; adult/child €7.50/4, audioguide €2; ⊗ 10am-12.30pm & 2-6.30pm Mon & Wed-Fri, 2-6.30pm Tue, 11am-6.30pm Sat & Sun mid-Apr–mid-Oct, to 6pm, closed Tue mid-Oct–mid-Apr) Jules Verne (1828–1905) wrote some of his best-known works of brain-tingling – and eerily prescient – science fiction under the eaves of this turreted home, where he

lived from 1882 to 1900. The 700 models, prints, posters and other items inspired by Verne's boundless imagination afford a fascinating opportunity to check out the future as he envisioned it over a century ago, when going around the world in 80 days sounded utterly fantastic.

Beffroi d'Amiens   TOWER
(place au Fil; belfry & cathedral tour adult/child €6/3, belfry only €4/2) Constructed between 1406 and 1410, Amiens' massive square belfry – a Unesco-listed monument – has a mid-18th-century top reaching 52m, which was rebuilt after it was damaged in 1940 by German bombing. The tourist office runs two guided tours per month, one including a cathedral tour, plus night-time visits in July and August – check the website and reserve well ahead.

Hortillonnages Cruises   BOATING
(☑ 03 22 92 12 18; http://leshortillonnages-amiens.fr; 54 bd Beauvillé; adult/child €6/5; ⊗ 9am-noon & 1.30-6pm Apr-Oct) Covering some 3 sq km, Amiens' market gardens have supplied the city with vegetables and flowers since the Middle Ages. Today, their peaceful *rieux* (waterways), home to seven working farms, more than 1000 private gardens and countless water birds, can be visited on tours aboard gondola-like 12-person boats with raised prows.

From mid-June to mid-October, the Hortillonnages host contemporary art installations accessible on foot, by bicycle or by rental *barque* (boat).

Sleeping & Eating

Le Quatorze
B&B €

(☑ 06 16 89 19 87; www.lequatorze.fr; 14 av de Dublin; s/d incl breakfast €65/75; ☎) Laure offers the perfect B&B experience 1.5km southeast of the train station in the Quartier Anglais (English Quarter). The five rooms are full of old-time touches (original tiles, wooden flooring, marble fireplaces) spanning two floors. All have private bathrooms; two are across the hall from the rooms. Amenities include a guest kitchen, laundry facilities and a rambling English-style garden.

Hôtel Victor Hugo
HOTEL €

(☑ 03 22 91 57 91; www.hotel-a-amiens.fr; 2 rue de l'Oratoire; d from €52; ☎) This bargain-priced, family-run hotel has 10 simple but comfortable rooms. The best-value rooms – if you don't mind a long stair climb – are under the eaves on the top floor, offering rooftop views and streaming natural light.

★ Hôtel Marotte
BOUTIQUE HOTEL €€

(☑ 03 60 12 50 00; www.hotel-marotte.com; 3 rue Marotte; d/q from €166/325; P ✲ ☎) Modern French luxury is at its most romantic at this boutique hotel. All 12 light-drenched rooms are huge (at least 35 sq metres), but the two sauna suites (100 sq metres), sporting free-standing stone bathtubs weighing 1.5 tonnes, are really luxury apartments; one opens to a rooftop terrace.

Grand Hôtel de l'Univers
HOTEL €€

(☑ 03 22 91 52 51; www.hotel-univers-amiens.com; 2 rue de Noyon; d €95-125; @ ☎) Built in 1875, this venerable, Best Western–affiliated hostelry has a superb parkside location. The 40 sound-proofed rooms, set around a three-storey atrium, are immaculate and very comfortable; those on the 2nd floor come with balconies. Spacious corner rooms such as room 26 are flooded with natural light.

Le Tire Bouchon
FRENCH €

(☑ 06 83 52 58 42; www.facebook.com/letirebouchon80; 1 bd du Cange; 2-/3-course menus €16/19, mains €12.50-16, sharing plates €3-11; ☺ kitchen 11.30am-3pm & 6.30-10.30pm, bar 11.30am-midnight Sun-Thu, to 1am Fri, to 3am Sat) With a table-filled riverside terrace, this contemporary wine bar is ideal for a drink and small sharing plate such as bone marrow with lemon zest, duck and fig terrine or sardine rillettes with capers, but it also has more substantial dishes such as steak tartare or the house special burger with Somme-produced Rollot cheese. Live music, especially blues and jazz, plays on weekends.

ⓘ Information

Tourist Office (☑ 03 22 71 60 50; www.visit-amiens.com; 23 place Notre Dame; ☺ 9.30am-6.30pm Mon-Sat, 10am-noon & 2-5pm Sun Apr-Sep, 9.30am-6pm Mon-Sat, 10am-noon & 2-5pm Sun Oct-Mar; ☎)

ⓘ Getting Around

Amiens' **Vélam** (☑ 08 20 20 02 99; www.velam.amiens.fr; subscription per day €1, 1st 30min free, per subsequent 30 min €1) bike-sharing scheme has 26 bike stations around town.

ROAD TRIP ESSENTIALS

France Driving Guide

With stunning landscapes, superb highways and one of the world's most scenic and comprehensive secondary road networks, France is a road-tripper's dream come true.

DRIVING LICENCE & DOCUMENTS

Drivers must carry the following at all times:

➜ passport or an EU national ID card

➜ valid driving licence (*permis de conduire;* most foreign licences can be used in France for up to a year)

➜ car-ownership papers, known as a *carte grise* (grey card)

➜ proof of third-party liability *assurance* (insurance)

An International Driving Permit (IDP) is not required when renting a car but can be useful in the event of an accident or police stop, as it translates and vouches for the authenticity of your home licence.

INSURANCE

Third-party liability insurance *(assurance au tiers)* is compulsory for all vehicles in France, including cars brought in from abroad. Normally, cars registered and insured in other European countries can circulate freely in France, but it's a good idea to contact your insurance company before you leave home to make sure you have coverage – and to check who to contact in case of a breakdown or accident.

If you get into a minor accident with no injuries, the easiest way for drivers to sort things out with their insurance companies is to fill out a Constat Aimable d'Accident Automobile (European Accident State-ment), a standardised way of recording important details about what happened. In rental cars it's usually in the packet of documents in the glove compartment. Make sure the report includes any information that will help you prove that the accident was not your fault. Remember, if it *was* your fault you may be liable for a hefty insurance deductible/excess. Don't sign anything you don't fully understand. If problems crop up, call the police (☑17).

French-registered cars have details of their insurance company printed on a little green square affixed to the windscreen.

HIRING A CAR

To hire a car in France, you'll generally need to be over 21 years old, have had a driving licence for at least a year, and have an international credit card. Drivers under 25 usually have to pay a surcharge *(frais jeune conducteur)* of €25 to €35 per day.

> ### Driving Fast Facts
>
> **Right or left?** Drive on the right
>
> **Manual or automatic?** Manual
>
> **Legal driving age** 18
>
> **Top speed limit** 130km/h on *autoroutes* (highways, motorways)
>
> **Signature car** Citroën 2CV

Road Trip Websites

AUTOMOBILE ASSOCIATIONS

RAC (www.rac.co.uk/driving-abroad/france) Info for British drivers on driving in France.

CONDITIONS & TRAFFIC

Bison Futé (www.bison-fute.gouv.fr)

Les Sociétés d'Autoroutes (www.autoroutes.fr)

ROUTE MAPPING

Mappy (www.mappy.fr)

Via Michelin (www.viamichelin.com)

Car-hire companies provide mandatory third-party liability insurance, but things such as collision-damage waivers (CDW, or *assurance tous risques*) vary greatly from company to company. When comparing rates and conditions (ie the fine print), the most important thing to check is the *franchise* (deductible/excess), which for a small car is usually around €600 for damage and €800 for theft. With many companies, you can reduce the excess by half, and perhaps to zero, by paying a daily insurance supplement of up to €20. Your credit card may cover CDW if you use it to pay for the rental, but the car-hire company won't know anything about this – verify conditions and details with your credit-card issuer to be sure.

Arranging your car hire or fly/drive package before you leave home is usually considerably cheaper than a walk-in rental, but beware of website offers that don't include a CDW or you may be liable for up to 100% of the car's value.

International car-hire companies:

Avis (www.avis.com)

Budget (www.budget.fr)

EasyCar (www.easycar.com)

Europcar (www.europcar.com)

Hertz (www.hertz.com)

Sixt (www.sixt.fr)

French car-hire companies:

ADA (www.ada.fr)

DLM (www.dlm.fr)

France Cars (www.francecars.fr)

Locauto (www.locauto.fr)

Renault Rent (www.renault-rent.com)

Rent a Car (www.rentacar.fr)

Deals can be found on the internet and through companies such as the following:

Auto Europe (www.autoeurope.com)

DriveAway Holidays (www.driveaway.com.au)

Holiday Autos (www.holidayautos.co.uk)

Rental cars with automatic transmission are very much the exception in France; they usually need to be ordered well in advance and are more expensive than manual cars.

For insurance reasons, it is usually forbidden to take rental cars on ferries, eg to Corsica.

All rental cars registered in France have a distinctive number on the licence plate, making them easily identifiable – including to thieves. *Never* leave anything of value in a parked car, even in the boot (trunk).

BRINGING YOUR OWN VEHICLE

Any foreign motor vehicle entering France must display a sticker or licence plate identifying its country of registration. Right-hand-drive vehicles brought from the UK or Ireland must have deflectors affixed to the headlights to avoid dazzling oncoming traffic.

MAPS

Michelin's excellent, detailed regional driving maps are highly recommended as a driving companion, as they will help you navigate back roads and explore alternative routes. Look for both at newsagents, bookshops, airports, supermarkets, tourist offices and service stations along the autoroute.

Institut Géographique National (IGN; www.ign.fr) Publishes regional fold-out maps as well as an all-France volume, *France – Routes, Autoroutes*.

Michelin (www.michelin-boutique.com) Sells excellent, tear-proof yellow-orange 1:200,000-scale regional maps tailor-made for cross-country driving, with precise coverage of smaller back roads.

ROADS & CONDITIONS

France has one of Europe's densest highway networks. There are four types of intercity roads:

Autoroutes (Highway names beginning with A) Multilane divided highways, usually (except near Calais and Lille) with tolls (*péages*). Generously outfitted with rest stops.

Routes Nationales (N, RN) National highways. Some sections have divider strips.

Routes Départementales (D) Local highways and roads.

Routes Communales (C, V) Minor rural roads.

The latter two categories, while slower, offer some of France's most enjoyable driving experiences.

Motorcyclists will find France great for touring, with high-quality roads and stunning scenery. Just make sure your wet-weather gear is up to scratch.

Note that high mountain passes, especially in the Alps, may be closed from as early as September to as late as June. Conditions are posted at the foot of each pass ('*ouvert*' on a green background means open, '*ferme*' on a red background means closed). Snow chains or studded tyres are required in wintry weather.

Driving Problem-Buster

I can't speak French; will that be a problem? While it's preferable to learn some French before travelling, French road signs are mostly of the 'international symbol' variety, and English is increasingly spoken among the younger generation.

What should I do if my car breaks down? Safety first: turn on your flashers, put on a safety vest (legally required, and provided in rental-car glove compartments) and place a reflective triangle (also legally required) 30m to 100m behind your car to warn approaching motorists. Call for emergency assistance (112) or walk to the nearest orange roadside call box (placed every 2km along French *autoroutes*). If renting a vehicle, your car-hire company's service number may help expedite matters. If travelling in your own car, verify before leaving home whether your local auto club has reciprocal roadside-assistance arrangements in France.

What if I have an accident? For minor accidents you'll need to fill out a *constat amiable d'accident* (accident statement, typically provided in rental-car glove compartments) and report the accident to your insurance and/or rental-car company. If necessary, contact the police (⏎17).

What should I do if I get stopped by the police? Show your passport (or EU national ID card), licence and proof of insurance.

What's the speed limit in France and how is it enforced? Speed limits (indicated by a black-on-white number inside a red circle) range from 30km/h in small towns to 130km/h on the fastest *autoroutes*. If the motorbike police pull you over, they'll fine you on the spot or direct you to the nearest gendarmerie to pay. If you're caught by a speed camera (placed at random intervals along French highways), the ticket will be sent to your rental-car agency, which will bill your credit card, or to your home address if you're driving your own vehicle. Fines depend on how much you're over the limit.

How do French tolls work? Many French *autoroutes* charge tolls. Take a ticket from the machine upon entering the highway and pay as you exit. Some exit booths are staffed by people; others are automated and will accept only chip-and-PIN credit cards or coins.

ROAD RULES

Enforcement of French traffic laws (see www.securiteroutiere.gouv.fr) has been stepped up considerably in recent years. Speed cameras are common, as are radar traps and unmarked police vehicles. Fines for many infractions are given on the spot, and serious violations can lead to the confiscation of your driving licence and car.

Speed Limits

Enforcement of French traffic laws (see www.securiteroutiere.gouv.fr) has been stepped up considerably in recent years. Speed cameras are common, as are radar traps and unmarked police vehicles. Fines for many infractions are given on the spot, and serious violations can lead to the confiscation of your driving licence and car.

Speed limits outside built-up areas (except where signposted otherwise):

Undivided N and D highways 80km/h (70km/h when raining)

Non-autoroute divided highways 110km/h (100km/h when raining)

Autoroutes 130km/h (110km/h when raining, 60km/h in icy conditions)

To reduce carbon emissions, *autoroute* speed limits have recently been reduced to 110km/h in some areas.

Unless otherwise signposted, a limit of 50km/h applies in *all* areas designated as built up, no matter how rural they may appear. You must slow to 50km/h the moment you come to a white sign with a red border and a place name written on it; the speed limit applies until you pass an identical sign with a horizontal bar through it.

Road Distances (KM)

From	Bayonne	Bordeaux	Brest	Caen	Cahors	Calais	Chambéry	Cherbourg	Clermont-Ferrand	Dijon	Grenoble	Lille	Lyon	Marseille	Nantes	Nice	Paris	Perpignan	Strasbourg	Toulouse
Bordeaux	184																			
Brest	811	623																		
Caen	764	568	376																	
Cahors	307	218	788	661																
Calais	164	876	710	339	875															
Chambéry	860	651	120	800	523	834														
Cherbourg	835	647	399	124	743	461	923													
Clermont-Ferrand	564	358	805	566	269	717	295	689												
Dijon	807	619	867	548	378	572	273	671	279											
Grenoble	827	657	1126	806	501	863	56	929	300	302										
Lille	997	809	725	353	808	112	767	476	650	505	798									
Lyon	831	528	1018	698	439	755	103	820	171	194	110	687								
Marseille	700	651	1271	1010	521	1067	344	1132	477	506	273	999	314							
Nantes	513	326	298	292	491	593	780	317	462	656	787	609	618	975						
Nice	858	810	1429	1168	679	1225	410	1291	636	664	337	1157	473	190	1131					
Paris	771	583	596	232	582	289	565	355	424	313	571	222	462	775	384	932				
Perpignan	499	451	1070	998	320	1149	478	1094	441	640	445	1081	448	319	773	476	857			
Strasbourg	1254	1066	1079	730	847	621	496	853	584	335	551	522	488	803	867	804	490	935		
Toulouse	300	247	866	865	116	991	565	890	890	727	533	923	536	407	568	564	699	205	1022	
Tours	536	348	490	246	413	531	611	369	369	418	618	463	449	795	197	952	238	795	721	593

Priority to the Right

Under the *priorité à droite* ('priority to the right') rule, any car entering an intersection (including a T-junction) from a road (including a tiny village backstreet) on your right has the right of way. Locals assume every driver knows this, so don't be surprised if they courteously cede the right of way when you're about to turn from an alley onto a highway – and boldly assert their rights when you're the one zipping down a main road.

Priorité à droite is suspended (eg on arterial roads) when you pass a sign showing an upended yellow square with a black square in the middle. The same sign with a horizontal bar through the square lozenge reinstates the *priorité à droite* rule.

When you arrive at a roundabout at which you do not have the right of way (ie the cars already in the roundabout do), you'll often see signs reading *vous n'avez pas la priorité* (you do not have right of way) or *cédez le passage* (give way).

Alcohol

Blood-alcohol limit is 0.05% (0.5g per litre of blood) – the equivalent of two glasses of wine for a 75kg adult. Police often conduct random breathalyser tests and penalties can be severe, including imprisonment.

Motorcycles

Riders of any type of two-wheeled vehicle with a motor (except motor-assisted bicycles) must wear a helmet. No special licence is required to ride a motorbike whose engine is smaller than 50cc, which is why rental scooters are often rated at 49.9cc.

Child Seats

➡ Children under 10 are not permitted to ride in the front seat (unless the back is already occupied by other children under 10).

➡ A child under 13kg must travel in a backward-facing child seat (permitted in the front seat only for babies under 9kg and if the airbag is deactivated).

➡ Up to age 10 and/or a minimum height of 140cm, children must use a size-appropriate type of front-facing child seat or booster.

Other Rules

➡ All passengers, including those in the back seat, must wear seat belts.

➡ Mobile phones may be used only if they are equipped with a hands-free kit or speakerphone.

➡ Turning right on a red light is illegal.

➡ Cars from the UK and Ireland must have deflectors affixed to their headlights to avoid dazzling oncoming motorists.

➡ Radar detectors, even if they're switched off, are illegal; fines are hefty.

➡ All vehicles driven in France must carry a high-visibility reflective safety vest (stored inside the vehicle, not in the trunk/boot), a reflective triangle, and a portable, single-use breathalyser kit.

➡ If you'll be driving on snowy roads, make sure you have snow chains (*chaînes neige*), required by law whenever and wherever the police post signs.

PARKING

In city centres, most on-street parking places are *payant* (metered) from about 9am to 7pm (sometimes with a break from noon to 2pm) Monday to Saturday, except bank holidays.

FUEL

Essence (petrol), also known as *carburant* (fuel), costs between €1.48 and €1.65 per litre for 95 unleaded (Sans Plomb 95 or SP95, usually available from a green pump) and €1.35 to €1.60 for diesel (*diesel, gazole* or *gasoil,* usually available from a yellow pump). Check and compare current prices countrywide at www.prix-carburants.gouv.fr.

Filling up *(faire le plein)* is most expensive at *autoroute* rest stops, and usually cheapest at hypermarkets.

France Playlist

Bonjour Rachid Taha and Gaetan Roussel

Coeur Vagabond Gus Viseur

La Vie en Rose Édith Piaf

Minor Swing Django Reinhardt

L'Americano Akhenaton

Flower Duet from Lakmé Léo Delibes

De Bonnes Raisons Alex Beaupain

Many small petrol stations close on Sunday afternoons and, even in cities, it can be hard to find a staffed station open late at night. In general, after-hours purchases (eg at hypermarkets' fully automatic, 24-hour stations) can only be made with a credit card that has an embedded PIN chip (p114), so if all you've got is cash or a magnetic-strip credit card, you could be stuck.

SATELLITE NAVIGATION SYSTEMS

Sat-nav devices can be helpful in navigating your way around France. They're commonly available at car-rental agencies, or you can bring your own from home. Accuracy is more dependable on main highways than in small villages or on back roads; in rural areas, don't hesitate to fall back on common sense, road signs and a good Michelin map if your sat nav seems to be leading you astray.

SAFETY

Never leave anything valuable inside your car, even in the boot (trunk). Note that thieves can easily identify rental cars, as they have a distinctive number on the licence plate.

Theft is especially prevalent in the south. In cities such as Marseille and Nice, occasional aggressive theft from cars stopped at red lights is also an issue.

RADIO

For news, tune in to the French-language France Info (105.5MHz; www.franceinfo. fr), multilanguage RFI (738kHz or 89MHz in Paris; www.rfi.fr) or, in northern France, the BBC World Service (648kHz) and BBC Radio 4 (198kHz). Popular national FM music stations include NRJ (www.nrj. fr), Virgin (www.virginradio.fr), La Radio Plus (www.laradioplus.com) and Nostalgie (www.nostalgie.fr).

In many areas, Autoroute Info (107.7MHz) has round-the-clock traffic information.

France
Travel Guide

GETTING THERE & AWAY

Flights, cars and tours can be booked online at www.lonelyplanet.com/bookings.

AIR

Air France (www.airfrance.com) is the national carrier, with plenty of both domestic and international flights in and out of major French airports.

Smaller provincial airports with international flights, mainly to/from the UK, continental Europe and North Africa, include Paris-Beauvais, Bergerac, Biarritz, Brest, Brive-la-Gaillarde (Vallée de la Dordogne), Caen, Carcassonne, Clermont-Ferrand, Deauville, Dinard, Grenoble, La Rochelle, Le Touquet (Côte d'Opale), Limoges, Montpellier, Nîmes, Pau, Perpignan, Poitiers, Rennes, Rodez, St-Étienne, Toulon and Tours.

Aéroport de Charles de Gaulle, Paris (CDG; ☑01 70 36 39 50; www.parisaeroport.fr)

Aéroport d'Orly, Paris (ORY; ☑01 70 36 39 50; www.parisaeroport.fr)

Aéroport de Bordeaux (Bordeaux Airport; BOD; ☑Information 05 56 34 50 50; www.bordeaux.aeroport.fr; Mérignac)

Aéroport de Lille (LIL; www.lille.aeroport.fr; rte de L'Aéroport, Lesquin)

Aéroport International Strasbourg (SXB; www.strasbourg.aeroport.fr)

Aéroport Lyon-St Exupéry (LYS; www.lyonaeroports.com)

Aéroport Marseille-Provence (Aéroport Marseille-Marignane; MRS; ☑08 20 81 14 14; www.marseille.aeroport.fr)

Aéroport Montpellier (MPL; ☑04 67 20 85 00; www.montpellier.aeroport.fr)

Aéroport Nantes Atlantique (NTE; www.nantes.aeroport.fr)

Aéroport Nice-Côte d'Azur (NCE; ☑08 20 42 33 33; www.nice.aeroport.fr; ☎; ☐98, 99, ☐2)

Aéroport Toulouse-Blagnac (TLS; www.toulouse.aeroport.fr/en)

EuroAirport, Basel (MLH or BSL; ☑+33 3 89 90 31 11; www.euroairport.com)

CAR & MOTORCYCLE

A right-hand-drive vehicle brought to France from the UK or Ireland must have deflectors affixed to the headlights to avoid dazzling oncoming traffic. In the UK, information on driving in France is available from the RAC (www.rac.co.uk/driving-abroad/france) and the AA (www.theaa.com).

A foreign motor vehicle entering France must display a sticker or licence plate identifying its country of registration.

Eurotunnel

The Channel Tunnel (Chunnel), inaugurated in 1994, is the first dry-land link between England and France since the last ice age.

High-speed **Eurotunnel Le Shuttle** (☑France 08 10 63 03 04, UK 08443 35 35 35; www.eurotunnel.com) trains whisk bicycles, motorcycles, cars and coaches in 35 minutes from Folkestone through the Channel Tunnel to Coquelles, 5km southwest of Calais. Shuttles run 24 hours a day, with up to three departures an hour during peak periods. LPG and CNG tanks are not permitted, meaning gas-powered cars and many campers and caravans have to travel by ferry.

Eurotunnel sets its fares the way budget airlines do: the further in advance you book and the lower the demand for a particular crossing, the less you pay; same-day fares can cost a small fortune. Fares for a car, including up to nine passengers, start at £30 (€37).

SEA

Some ferry companies have started setting fares the way budget airlines do: the longer in advance you book and the lower the demand for a particular sailing, the less you pay. Seasonal demand is a crucial factor (Christmas, Easter, UK and French school holidays, and July and August are especially busy), as is the time of day (an early-evening ferry can cost much more than one at 4am). People under 25 and over 60 may qualify for discounts.

To get the best fares, check Ferry Savers (www.ferrysavers.com).

Foot passengers are not allowed on Dover–Boulogne, Dover–Dunkirk or Dover–Calais car ferries except for daytime (and, from Calais to Dover, evening) crossings run by P&O Ferries. On ferries that do allow foot passengers, taking a bicycle is usually free.

Several ferry companies ply the waters between Corsica and Italy.

TRAIN

Rail services link France with virtually every country in Europe.

➡ Book tickets and get train information from Rail Europe (www.raileurope.com). In the UK contact Railteam (www.railteam.co.uk).

➡ A very useful train-travel resource is the information-packed website The Man in Seat 61 (www.seat61.com).

Certain rail services between France and its continental neighbours are marketed under unique brand names:

Elipsos Luxurious, overnight 'train-hotel' from Paris to Madrid and Barcelona in Spain; book through France's **SNCF** (Société Nationale des Chemins de fer Français, French National Railway Company; ☎from abroad +33 8 92 35 35 35, in France 36 35; http://en.voyages-sncf.com).

TGV Lyria (high-speed train; www.tgv-lyria.fr) To Switzerland.

Thalys (www.thalys.com) Thalys trains pull into Paris' Gare du Nord from Brussels, Amsterdam and Cologne.

Thello (www.thello.com) Overnight train service from Paris to Milan, Brescia, Verona and Venice in Italy.

DIRECTORY A–Z

ACCESSIBLE TRAVEL

While France presents evident challenges for *visiteurs handicapés* (disabled visitors), particularly those with mobility issues – cobblestones, cafe-lined streets that are a nightmare to navigate in a wheelchair *(fauteuil roulant)*, a lack of kerb ramps, older public facilities and many budget hotels without lifts – don't let that stop you from visiting. Efforts are being made to improve the situation and with a little careful planning, a hassle-free accessible stay is possible.

➡ Paris' tourist office runs the excellent 'Tourisme & Handicap' initiative whereby museums, cultural attractions, hotels and restaurants that provide access or special assistance or facilities for those with physical, mental, visual and/or hearing disabilities display a special logo at their entrances. For a list of qualifying places, go to www.parisinfo.com and click on 'Practical Paris'.

➡ Paris metro, most of it built decades ago, is hopeless. Line 14 of the metro was built to be wheelchair-accessible, although in reality it remains extremely challenging to navigate in a wheelchair – unlike Paris buses which are 100% accessible.

➡ Parisian taxi company Horizon, part of Taxis G7 (www.taxisg7.fr), has cars especially adapted to carry wheelchairs and drivers trained in helping passengers with disabilities.

➡ Countrywide, many SNCF train carriages are accessible to people with disabilities. A traveller in a wheelchair can travel in both the TGV and in the 1st-class carriage with a 2nd-class ticket on mainline trains provided they make a reservation by phone or at a train station at least a few hours before departure. Details are available in the SNCF booklet *Le Mémento du Voyageur Handicapé* (Handicapped Traveller Summary) available at all train stations.

Practicalities

Laundry Virtually all French cities and towns have at least one laverie libre-service (self-service laundrette). Machines run on coins.

Newspapers and magazines Locals read their news in centre-left *Le Monde* (www.lemonde.fr), right-leaning *Le Figaro* (www.lefigaro.fr) or left-leaning *Libération* (www.liberation.fr).

Radio For news, tune in to the French-language France Info (105.5MHz; www.franceinfo.fr) and multilanguage RFI (738kHz or 89MHz in Paris; www.rfi.fr). Popular national FM music stations include NRJ (www.nrj.fr), Virgin (www.virginradio.fr), La Radio Plus (www.laradioplus.com) and Nostalgie (www.nostalgie.fr).

Smoking Illegal in all indoor public spaces, including restaurants and pubs (though, of course, smokers still light up on the terraces outside).

Weights and measures France uses the metric system.

Resources

Accès Plus (☑03 69 32 26 26, 08 90 64 06 50; www.accessibilite.sncf.com) The SNCF assistance service for rail travellers with disabilities. Can advise on station accessibility and arrange a *fauteuil roulant* or help getting on or off a train.

Access Travel (☑UK 07973 114 365; www.access-travel.co.uk) Specialised UK-based agency for accessible travel.

Infomobi.com (☑09 70 81 93 95; www.vianavigo.com/accessibilite) Has comprehensive information on accessible travel in Paris and the surrounding Île de France area.

Mobile en Ville (☑09 52 29 60 51; www.mobileenville.org; 8 rue des Mariniers, 14e) Association that works hard to make independent travel within Paris easier for people in wheelchairs. Among other things it organises some great family *randonnées* (walks) in and around Paris.

Tourisme et Handicaps (☑01 44 11 10 41; www.tourisme-handicaps.org; 43 rue Marx Dormoy, 18e) Issues the 'Tourisme et Handicap' label to tourist sites, restaurants and hotels that comply with strict accessibility and usability standards. Different symbols indicate the sort of access afforded to people with physical, mental, hearing and/or visual disabilities.

ACCOMMODATION

Categories

As a rule of thumb, budget covers everything from basic hostels to small family-run places; midrange means a few extra creature comforts such as a lift; while top-end places stretch from luxury five-star palaces with air-conditioning, swimming pools and restaurants to boutique-chic Alpine chalets.

Costs

Accommodation costs vary wildly between seasons and regions: what will buy you a night in a romantic *chambre d'hôte* (B&B) in the countryside may get a dorm bed in a major city or high-profile ski resort.

Reservations

Midrange, top-end and many budget hotels require a credit card number to secure an advance reservation made by phone; some hostels do not take bookings. Many tourist offices can advise on availability and reserve for you, often for a fee of €5 and usually only if you stop by in person. In the Alps, ski-resort tourist offices run a central reservation service for booking accommodation.

B&Bs

For charm, a heartfelt *bienvenue* (welcome) and solid home cooking, it's hard to beat France's privately run *chambres*

Sleeping Price Ranges

The following price ranges refer to a double room in high season, with private bathroom (any combination of toilet, bathtub, shower and washbasin), excluding breakfast unless otherwise noted. Breakfast is assumed to be included at a B&B. Where half-board (breakfast and dinner) and full board (breakfast, lunch and dinner) is included, this is mentioned with the price.

€ less than €90 (less than €130 in Paris)

€€ €90–190 (€130–250 in Paris)

€€€ more than €190 (more than €250 in Paris)

d'hôte (B&Bs) – urban rarities but as common as muck in rural areas. By law a chambre d'hôte must have no more than five rooms and breakfast must be included in the price; some hosts prepare a meal (table d'hôte) for an extra charge of around €30 including wine. Pick up lists of chambres d'hôte at tourist offices, or find one to suit online.

Bienvenue à la Ferme (www.bienvenue-a-la-ferme.com) Farmstay accommodation options for a taste of French rural life.

Chambres d'Hôtes France (www.chambresdhotesfrance.com) Comprehensive, France-wide B&B listings.

Fleurs de Soleil (www.fleursdesoleil.fr) Selective collection of 550 stylish maisons d'hôte, mainly in rural France.

Gîtes de France (www.gites-de-france.com) France's primary umbrella organisation for B&Bs and self-catering properties (gîtes); search by region, theme (charm, with kids, by the sea, gourmet, great garden etc.), activity (fishing, wine tasting etc) or facilities (pool, dishwasher, fireplace, baby equipment etc).

iGuide Rivages (www.iguide-hotels.com) Gorgeous presentation of France's most charming and often-times most upmarket B&Bs, organised by region and/or theme (romantic, gastronomic, green, oenological and so forth).

Samedi Midi Éditions (www.samedimidi.com) Country, mountain, seaside...choose your chambre d'hôte by location or theme (romance, golf, design, cooking courses).

Camping

Be it a Mongolian yurt, boutique tree house or simple canvas beneath stars, camping in France is in vogue. Thousands of well-equipped campgrounds dot the country,

many considerably placed by rivers, lakes and the sea.

➡ Most campgrounds open March or April to late September or October; popular spots fill up fast in summer so it is wise to call ahead.

➡ 'Sites' refer to fixed-price deals for two people including a tent and a car. Otherwise the price is broken down per adult/tent/car. Factor in a few extra euro per night for taxe de séjour (holiday tax) and electricity.

➡ Euro-economisers should look out for local, good-value but no-frills campings municipaux (municipal campgrounds).

➡ Many campgrounds rent out mobile homes with mod cons such as heating, fitted kitchen and TV.

➡ Pitching up 'wild' in nondesignated spots (camping sauvage) is illegal in France.

➡ Campground offices often close during the day.

➡ Accessing many campgrounds without your own transport can be slow and costly, or simply impossible.

Websites with campsite listings searchable by location, theme and facilities:

Bienvenue à la Ferme (www.bienvenue-a-la-ferme.com)

Camping en France (www.camping.fr)

Camping France (www.campingfrance.com)

Gîtes de France (www.gites-de-france.com)

HPA Guide (http://camping.hpaguide.com)

Glamping

Farewell clammy canvas, adieu inflatable mattress... Glamping in France is cool and creative, with écolo chic (ecochic) and adventurous alternatives springing up all the time. If you fancy doing a Robinson Crusoe by staying in a tree house with an incredible view over the treetops, visit Cabanes de France (www.cabanes-de-france.com), which covers leafy options between branches all over France. Prefer to keep your feet firmly on the ground? Keep an eye out for ecoconscious campsites where you can snooze in a *tipi* (tepee) or in a giant hammock.

Homestays

One of the best ways to brush up your *français* and immerse yourself in local life is by staying with a French family under an arrangement known as *hôtes payants* or *hébergement chez l'habitant*. Popular among students and young people, this set-up means you rent a room and usually have access (sometimes limited) to the bathroom and the kitchen; meals may also be available. If you are sensitive to smoke or pets, make sure you mention this.

Gîtes de France (www.gites-de-france.com) Handles some of the most charming *gîtes ruraux* (self-contained holiday cottages) in rural areas.

Homestay.com (www.homestay.com) Homestays in major French cities.

Hostels

Hostels in France range from funky to threadbare, although with a wave of design-driven, up-to-the-minute hostels opening in Paris, Marseille and other big cities, hip hang-outs with perks aplenty seem to easily outweigh the threadbare these days.

➡ In university towns, *foyers d'étudiant* (student dormitories) are sometimes converted for use by travellers during summer.

➡ A dorm bed in an *auberge de jeunesse* (hostel) costs €20 to €50 in Paris, and anything from €15 to €40 in the provinces, depending on location, amenities and facilities; sheets are always included, as is breakfast more often than not.

➡ To prevent outbreaks of bedbugs, sleeping bags are not permitted.

➡ Hostels by the sea or in the mountains sometimes offer seasonal outdoor activities.

➡ French hostels are 100% nonsmoking.

Hotels

Hotels in France are rated with one to five stars, although the ratings are based on highly objective criteria (eg the size of the

entry hall), not the quality of the service, the decor or cleanliness.

➡ French hotels almost never include breakfast in their rates. Unless specified otherwise, prices quoted don't include breakfast, which costs around €8/12/25 in a budget/midrange/top-end hotel.

➡ When you book, hotels usually ask for a credit card number; some require a deposit.

➡ A double room generally has one double bed (sometimes two singles pushed together!); a room with twin beds *(deux lits)* is usually more expensive, as is a room with a bathtub instead of a shower.

➡ Feather pillows are practically nonexistent in France, even in top-end hotels.

➡ All hotel restaurant terraces allow smoking; if you are sensitive to smoke, you may need to sit inside.

Rental Accommodation

If you are planning on staying put for more than a few days or are travelling in a group, then renting a furnished studio, apartment or villa can be an economical alternative. You will have the chance to live like a local, with trips to the farmers market and the *boulangerie* (bakery).

Finding an apartment for long-term rental can be gruelling. Landlords, many of whom prefer locals to foreigners, usually require substantial proof of financial responsibility and sufficient funds in France; many ask for a *caution* (guarantee) and a hefty deposit.

➡ Cleaning, linen rental and electricity fees usually cost extra.

➡ Classified ads appear in *De Particulier à Particulier* (www.pap.fr, in French), published on Thursday and sold at news stands.

➡ For apartments outside Paris it's best to search at your destination.

Book Your Stay Online

For more accommodation reviews by Lonely Planet authors, check out http://lonelyplanet.com/france/hotels/. You'll find independent reviews, as well as recommendations on the best places to stay. Best of all, you can book online.

→ Check places like bars and *tabacs* (tobacconists) for free local newspapers (often named after the number of the *département*) with classifieds listings.

ELECTRICITY

Type C
220V/50Hz

Type E
230V/50Hz

FOOD

It pays to know what and how much to eat, and when – adopting the local culinary pace is key to savouring every last exquisite moment of the French day.

Petit déjeuner (breakfast) The French kick-start the day with a tartine (slice of baguette smeared with unsalted butter and jam) and *un café* (espresso), long milky *café au lait* or – especially for kids – hot chocolate. In hotels you get a real cup but in French homes, coffee and hot chocolate are drunk from a cereal bowl – perfect bread-dunking terrain. Croissants (eaten straight, never with butter or jam) are a weekend treat along with brioches (sweet breads), *pains au chocolat* (chocolate-filled croissants) and other *viennoiserie* (sweet baked goods).

Déjeuner (lunch) A meal few French would go without. The traditional main meal of the day, lunch translates as a starter and main course with wine, followed by an espresso. Sunday lunch is a long, languid affair taking several hours. Indeed, a fully fledged, traditional French meal – *déjeuner* or *dîner* – can comprise six courses, each accompanied by a different wine. Standard restaurant lunch hours are noon to 2.30pm.

Aperitif The *apéro* (predinner drink) is sacred. Urban cafes and bars get packed out from around 5pm onwards as workers relax over a chit-chat-fuelled *kir* (white wine sweetened with blackcurrant syrup), glass of red or beer. Come weekends, a leisurely noon-time *apéro* before lunch is equally acceptable – and oh so pleasurable.

Goûter An afternoon snack, devoured with particular relish by French children. A slab of

Eating Price Ranges

Price indicators refer to the average cost of a two-course meal, be it an *entrée* (starter) and *plat* (main course) or main and dessert, or a two- or three-course *menu* (set meal at a fixed price).

€ less than €20

€€ €20–40

€€€ more than €40

milk chocolate inside a wedge of baguette is a traditional favourite.

Dîner (dinner) Traditionally lighter than lunch, but a meal that is increasingly treated as the main meal of the day. Standard restaurant times are 7pm to 10.30pm.

INSURANCE

➤ Comprehensive travel insurance to cover theft, loss and medical problems is highly recommended.

➤ Some policies specifically exclude dangerous activities such as scuba diving, motorcycling, skiing and even trekking: read the fine print.

➤ Check that the policy covers ambulances or an emergency flight home.

➤ Find out in advance if your insurance plan will make payments directly to providers or reimburse you later for overseas health expenditures.

➤ If you have to claim later, make sure you keep all documentation.

➤ Paying for your airline ticket with a credit card often provides limited travel accident insurance – ask your credit card company what it is prepared to cover.

➤ Worldwide travel insurance is available at www.lonelyplanet.com/travel-insurance. You can buy, extend and claim online anytime – even if you're already on the road.

INTERNET ACCESS

➤ Wi-fi (pronounced 'wee-fee' in French) is available at major airports, in most hotels, and at many cafes, restaurants, museums and tourist offices.

➤ In cities free wi-fi is available in hundreds of public places, including parks, libraries and municipal buildings. In Paris look for a purple 'Zone Wi-Fi' sign. To connect, select the 'PARIS_WI-FI_' network. Sessions are limited to two hours (renewable). For complete details and a map of hotspots, see www.paris.fr/wifi.

➤ To search for free wi-fi hotspots in France, visit www.hotspot-locations.com.

➤ Tourist offices is some larger cities, including Lyon and Bordeaux, rent out pocket-sized mobile wi-fi devices that you carry around

with you, ensuring a fast wi-fi connection while roaming the city.

➤ Alternatively, rent a mobile wi-fi device online before leaving home and arrange for it to be delivered by post to your hotel in France through HipPocketWifi (http://hippocketwifi.com), Travel WiFi (http://travel-wifi.com) or My Webspot (http://my-webspot.com).

➤ Co-working cafes providing unlimited, fast internet access are increasingly rife; at least one can usually be tracked down in cities. Expect to pay about €5 per hour for a desk, plug and unlimited hot drinks and snacks.

LEGAL MATTERS

➤ French police have wide powers of search and seizure and can ask you to prove your identity at any time – whether or not there is 'probable cause'.

➤ Foreigners must be able to prove their legal status in France (eg with a passport, visa or residency permit) without delay.

➤ If the police stop you for any reason, be polite and remain calm. Verbally (and of course physically) abusing a police officer can lead to a hefty fine, and even imprisonment.

➤ You may refuse to sign a police statement, and have the right to ask for a copy.

➤ People who are arrested are considered innocent until proven guilty, but can be held in custody until trial.

Drugs & Alcohol

➤ French law does not distinguish between 'hard' and 'soft' drugs.

➤ The penalty for any personal use of *stupéfiants* (including cannabis, amphetamines, ecstasy and heroin) can be a one-year jail sentence and a €3750 fine but, depending on the circumstances, it might be anything from a stern word to a compulsory rehab program.

➤ Importing, possessing, selling or buying drugs can get you up to 10 years in prison and a fine of up to €500,000.

➤ Police have been known to search chartered coaches, cars and train passengers for drugs just because they're coming from Amsterdam.

➤ *Ivresse* (drunkenness) in public is punishable by a fine.

LGBT+ TRAVELLERS

The rainbow flag flies high in France, a country that left its closet long before many of its European neighbours. *Laissez-faire* perfectly sums up France's liberal attitude towards homosexuality and people's private lives in general; in part because of a long tradition of public tolerance towards unconventional lifestyles.

➜ Paris has been a thriving gay and lesbian centre since the late 1970s, and most major organisations are based there today.

➜ Bordeaux, Lille, Lyon, Montpellier, Toulouse and many other towns also have an active queer scene.

➜ Attitudes to homosexuality tend to be more conservative in the countryside and villages.

➜ France's lesbian scene is less public than its gay male counterpart and is centred mainly on women's cafes and bars.

➜ Same-sex marriage has been legal in France since May 2013.

➜ Gay Pride marches are held in major French cities mid-May to early July.

MONEY

ATMs

Automated Teller Machines (ATMs) – known as *distributeurs automatiques de billets* (DAB) or *points d'argent* in French – are the cheapest and most convenient way to get money. ATMs connected to international networks are situated in all cities and towns and usually offer an excellent exchange rate.

Cash

You always get a better exchange rate in-country, but it is a good idea to arrive in France with enough euros to take a taxi to a hotel if you have to.

➜ Commercial banks charge up to €5 per foreign-currency transaction – if they even bother to offer exchange services any more.

➜ In Paris and major cities, *bureaux de change* (exchange bureaus) are faster and easier, open longer hours and often give better rates than banks.

Credit & Debit Cards

➜ Credit and debit cards, accepted almost everywhere in France, are convenient, relatively secure and usually offer a better exchange rate than travellers cheques or cash exchanges.

➜ Credit cards issued in France have embedded chips – you have to type in a PIN to make a purchase.

➜ Visa, MasterCard and Amex can be used in shops and supermarkets and for train travel, car hire and motorway tolls.

➜ Don't assume that you can pay for a meal or a budget hotel with a credit card – enquire first.

➜ Cash advances are a supremely convenient way to stay stocked up with euros, but getting cash with a credit card involves both fees (sometimes US$10 or more) and interest – ask your credit-card issuer for details. Debit-card fees are usually much lower.

Exchange Rates

Australia	A$1	€0.64
Canada	C$1	€0.66
Japan	¥100	€0.76
NZ	NZ$1	€0.59
UK	UK£1	€1.14
USA	US$1	€0.85

For current exchange rates see www.xe.com.

Americans, Take Note

US-issued 'smart' credit/debit cards with embedded chips (a technology pioneered in France in the 1980s) and PINs work virtually everywhere in France, including autoroute toll plazas, but cards with a chip but no PIN may occasionally leave you unable to pay – for instance, at unstaffed, 24/7 petrol (gas) stations with self-pay pumps. If your credit card is of the old type, ie with a magnetic strip but no chip, ask your issuer to send you a new, chip-equipped card – they're usually happy to oblige as the new technology is much more secure.

Tipping

Hotels €1 to €2 per bag is standard; gratuity for cleaning staff completely at your discretion.

Bars No tips for drinks served at bar; round to nearest euro for drinks served at table.

Restaurants For decent service 10%.

Pubic toilets For super-clean, sparkling toilets with music, €0.50 at most.

Tours For excellent guides, €1 to €2 per person.

OPENING HOURS

Opening hours vary throughout the year. We list high-season opening hours, but remember these longer summer hours often decrease in shoulder and low seasons.

Banks 9am–noon and 2pm–5pm Monday to Friday or Tuesday to Saturday

Bars 7pm–1am

Cafes 7am–11pm

Clubs 10pm–3am, 4am or 5am Thursday to Saturday

Restaurants Noon–2.30pm and 7pm–11pm six days a week

Shops 10am–noon and 2pm–7pm Monday to Saturday; longer, and including Sunday, for shops in defined ZTIs (international tourist zones)

PUBLIC HOLIDAYS

The following *jours fériés* (public holidays) are observed in France:

New Year's Day (Jour de l'An) 1 January

Easter Sunday & Monday (Pâques & Lundi de Pâques) Late March/April

May Day (Fête du Travail) 1 May

Victoire 1945 8 May

Ascension Thursday (Ascension) May; on the 40th day after Easter

Pentecost/Whit Sunday & Whit Monday (Pentecôte & Lundi de Pentecôte) Mid-May to mid-June; on the seventh Sunday after Easter

Bastille Day/National Day (Fête Nationale) 14 July

Assumption Day (Assomption) 15 August

All Saints' Day (Toussaint) 1 November

Remembrance Day (L'onze Novembre) 11 November

Christmas (Noël) 25 December

The following are *not* public holidays in France: Shrove Tuesday (Mardi Gras; the first day of Lent); Maundy (or Holy) Thursday and Good Friday, just before Easter; and Boxing Day (26 December).

Note: Good Friday and Boxing Day *are* public holidays in Alsace.

TELEPHONE

Calling France from abroad Dial your country's international access code, then ⏏33 (France's country code), then the 10-digit local number *without* the initial zero.

Calling internationally from France Dial ⏏00 (the international access code), the *indicatif* (country code), the area code (without the initial zero if there is one) and the local number. Some country codes are posted in public telephones.

Directory enquiries For national *service des renseignements* (directory inquiries) dial ⏏11 87 12 or use the service for free online at www.118712.fr.

International directory inquiries For numbers outside France, dial ⏏11 87 00.

Mobile Phones

➡ French mobile phone numbers begin with ⏏06 or ⏏07.

➡ France uses GSM 900/1800, which is compatible with the rest of Europe and Australia but not with the North American GSM 1900 or the totally different system in Japan (though some North Americans have tri-band phones that work here).

➡ Check with your service provider about roaming charges – dialling a mobile phone from a fixed-line phone or another mobile can be incredibly expensive.

➡ It is usually cheaper to buy a local SIM card from a French provider such as Orange, SFR, Bouygues or Free Mobile, which gives you a local phone number. To do this, ensure your phone is unlocked.

➡ If you already have a compatible phone, you can slip in a SIM card and rev it up with prepaid credit, though this is likely to run out fast as domestic prepaid calls cost about €0.50 per minute.

➡ Recharge cards are sold at most *tabacs* (tobacconist-newsagents), supermarkets and online through websites such as Topengo (www.topengo.fr) or Sim-OK (https://recharge.sim-ok.com).

TOILETS

Public toilets, signposted WC or *toilettes*, are not always plentiful in France, especially outside the big cities.

Love them (as a sci-fi geek) or loathe them (as a claustrophobe), France's 24-hour self-cleaning toilets are here to stay. Outside Paris these mechanical WCs are free, but in Paris they cost around €0.50 a go. Don't even think about nipping in after someone else to avoid paying unless you fancy a *douche* (shower) with disinfectant. There is no time for dawdling either: you have precisely 15 minutes before being (ooh-la-la!) exposed to passers-by. Green means *libre* (vacant) and red means *occupé* (occupied).

Some older establishments and motorway stops still have the hole-in-the-floor *toilettes à la turque* (squat toilets). Provided you hover, these are actually very hygienic, but take care not to get soaked by the flush.

Keep some loose change handy for tipping toilet attendants, who keep a hawk-like eye on many of France's public toilets.

The French are completely blasé about unisex toilets, so save your blushes when tiptoeing past the urinals to reach the ladies' loo.

TOURIST INFORMATION

Almost every city, town and village has an *office de tourisme* (a tourist office run by some unit of local government) or *syndicat d'initiative* (a tourist office run by an organisation of local merchants). Both are excellent resources and can supply you with local maps as well as details on accommodation, restaurants and activities. If you have a special interest such as walking, cycling, architecture or wine sampling, ask about it.

➡ Many tourist offices make local hotel and B&B reservations, sometimes for a nominal fee.

➡ *Comités régionaux de tourisme* (CRTs; regional tourist boards), their *départemental* analogues (CDTs) and their websites are a superb source of information and hyperlinks.

➡ French government tourist offices (usually called Maisons de la France) provide every imaginable sort of tourist information on France.

Useful websites include the following:

French Government Tourist Office (www.france.fr/en) The low-down on sights, activities, transport and special-interest holidays in all of France's regions.

French Tourist Offices (www.tourisme. fr) Website of tourist offices in France, with mountains of inspirational information organised by theme and region.

TRAVEL WITH CHILDREN

In Paris and larger towns and cities, serviced apartments equipped with washing machine and kitchen are suited to families with younger children. Countrywide, hotels with family or four-person rooms can be hard to find and need booking in advance. Functional, if soulless, chain hotels such as Formule 1, found on the outskirts of most large towns, always have a generous quota of family rooms and make convenient overnight stops for motorists driving from continental Europe or the UK (Troyes is a popular stopover for Brits en route to the Alps). Parents with just one child and/or a baby in tow will have no problem finding hotel accommodation – most midrange hotels have baby cots and are happy to put a child's bed in a double room for a minimal extra cost.

In rural France, family-friendly B&Bs and *fermes auberges* (farm stays) are convenient. For older children, tree houses decked out with bunk beds and Mongolian yurts create a real family adventure.

Camping is huge with French families: check into a self-catering mobile home, wooden chalet or tent; sit back on the verandah with glass of wine in hand and watch as your kids – wonderfully oblivious to any barriers language might pose – run around with new-found French friends.

VISAS

➡ For up-to-date details on visa requirements, see the website of the **Ministère des Affaires Étrangères** (Ministry of Foreign Affairs; www.diplomatie.gouv.fr; 37 quai d'Orsay, 7e; ⓂAssemblée Nationale) and click 'Coming to France'.

➡ EU nationals and citizens of Iceland, Norway and Switzerland need only a passport or a national identity card to enter France and stay in the country, even for stays of more than 90 days. However, citizens of new EU member states may be subject to various limitations on living and working in France.

➡ Citizens of Australia, the USA, Canada, Hong Kong, Israel, Japan, Malaysia, New Zealand, Singapore, South Korea and many Latin American countries do not need visas to visit France as tourists for up to 90 days. For long stays of more than 90 days, contact your near-est French embassy or consulate and begin your application well in advance, as it can take months.

➡ Other people wishing to come to France as tourists have to apply for a Schengen Visa, named after the agreements that have abolished passport controls between 26 European countries. It allows unlimited travel throughout the entire zone for a 90-day period. Apply to the consulate of the country you are entering first, or your main destination. Among other things, you need travel and repatriation insurance and to be able to show that you have sufficient funds to support yourself.

➡ Tourist visas cannot be changed into student visas after arrival. However, short-term visas are available for students sitting university-entrance exams in France.

➡ Tourist visas cannot be extended except in emergencies (such as medical problems). When your visa expires you'll need to leave and reapply from outside France.

Language

The sounds used in spoken French can almost all be found in English. There are a couple of exceptions: nasal vowels (represented in our pronunciation guides by o or u followed by an almost inaudible nasal consonant sound m, n or ng), the 'funny' u (ew in our guides) and the deep-in-the-throat r. Bearing these few points in mind and reading our pronunciation guides below as if they were English, you'll be understood just fine.

BASICS

Hello.	*Bonjour.*	bon·zhoor
Goodbye.	*Au revoir.*	o·rer·vwa
Yes./No.	*Oui./Non.*	wee/non
Excuse me.	*Excusez-moi.*	ek·skew·zay·mwa
Sorry.	*Pardon.*	par·don
Please.	*S'il vous plaît.*	seel voo play
Thank you.	*Merci.*	mair·see

You're welcome.
De rien.   der ree·en

Do you speak English?
Parlez-vous anglais?   par·lay·voo ong·glay

I don't understand.
Je ne comprends pas.   zher ner kom·pron pa

How much is this?
C'est combien?   say kom·byun

ACCOMMODATION

Do you have any rooms available?
Est-ce que vous avez   es·ker voo za·vay
des chambres libres?   day shom·brer lee·brer

Want More?

For in-depth language information and handy phrases, check out Lonely Planet's *French Phrasebook*. You'll find it at **shop.lonelyplanet.com**, or you can buy Lonely Planet's iPhone phrasebooks at the Apple App Store.

How much is it per night/person?
Quel est le prix   kel ay ler pree
par nuit/personne?   par nwee/per·son

DIRECTIONS

Can you show me (on the map)?
Pouvez-vous m'indiquer   poo·vay·voo mun·dee·kay
(sur la carte)?   (sewr la kart)

Where's ...?
Où est ...?   oo ay ...

EATING & DRINKING

What would you recommend?
Qu'est-ce que vous   kes·ker voo
conseillez?   kon·say·yay

I'd like ..., please.
Je voudrais ...,   zher voo·dray ...
s'il vous plaît.   seel voo play

I'm a vegetarian.
Je suis végétarien/   zher swee vay·zhay·ta·ryun/
végétarienne.   vay·zhay·ta·ryen (m/f)

Please bring the bill.
Apportez-moi   a·por·tay·mwa
l'addition,   la·dee·syon
s'il vous plaît.   seel voo play

EMERGENCIES

Help!
Au secours!   o skoor

I'm lost.
Je suis perdu/perdue.   zhe swee·pair·dew (m/f)

I'm ill.
Je suis malade.   zher swee ma·lad

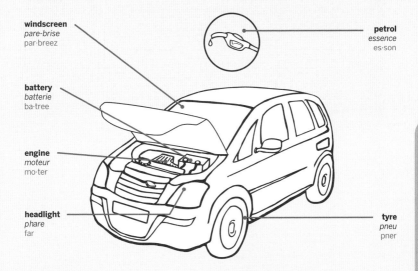

windscreen
pare-brise
par·breez

petrol
essence
es·son

battery
batterie
ba·tree

engine
moteur
mo·ter

headlight
phare
far

tyre
pneu
pner

Call the police!
Appelez la police!   a·play la po·lees

Call a doctor!
Appelez un médecin!   a·play un mayd·sun

ON THE ROAD

I'd like to hire a/an ...	*Je voudrais louer ...*	zher voo·dray loo·way ...
4WD	*un quatre-quatre*	un kat·kat
automatic/ manual	*une automatique/ manuel*	ewn o·to·ma·teek/ ma·nwel
motorbike	*une moto*	ewn mo·to

How much is it daily/weekly?
Quel est le tarif par jour/semaine?   kel ay ler ta·reef par zhoor/ser·men

Does that include insurance?
Est-ce que l'assurance est comprise?   es·ker la·sew·rons ay kom·preez

Does that include mileage?
Est-ce que le kilométrage est compris?   es·ker ler kee·lo·may·trazh ay kom·pree

What's the speed limit?
Quelle est la vitesse maximale permise?   kel ay la vee·tes mak·see·mal per·meez

Is this the road to ...?
C'est la route pour ...?   say la root poor ...

Can I park here?
Est-ce que je peux stationner ici?   es·ker zher per sta·syo·nay ee·see

Where's a service station?
Où est-ce qu'il y a une station-service?   oo es·keel ya ewn sta·syon·ser·vees

Please fill it up.
Le plein, s'il vous plaît.   ler plun seel voo play

I'd like (20) litres.
Je voudrais (vingt) litres.   zher voo·dray (vung) lee·trer

Please check the oil/water.
Contrôlez l'huile/l'eau, s'il vous plaît.   kon·tro·lay lweel/lo seel voo play

I need a mechanic.
J'ai besoin d'un mécanicien.   zhay ber·zwun dun may·ka·nee·syun

The car/motorbike has broken down.
La voiture/moto est tombée en panne.   la vwa·tewr/mo·to ay tom·bay on pan

I had an accident.
J'ai eu un accident.   zhay ew un ak·see·don

Signs

Cédez la Priorité	Give Way
Sens Interdit	No Entry
Entrée	Entrance
Péage	Toll
Sens Unique	One Way
Sortie	Exit

BEHIND THE SCENES

ACKNOWLEDGMENTS

Climate map data adapted from Peel MC, Finlayson BL & McMahon TA (2007) 'Updated World Map of the Köppen-Geiger Climate Classification', *Hydrology and Earth System Sciences,* 11, 163344.

Cover photographs: Front: Honfleur, JeniFoto/ Shutterstock ©; Back: Poppies on the Battlefields of the Somme, martb/Getty ©

THIS BOOK

This 2nd edition of *Normandy & D-Day Beaches Road Trips* was researched and written by Damian Harper and Catherine Le Nevez. This guidebook was produced by the following:

Destination Editor Daniel Fahey

Senior Product Editor Genna Patterson

Product Editor Kate Mathews

Editors Andrea Dobbin, Carly Hall, Victoria Harrison

Senior Cartographer Mark Griffiths

Cartographer Julie Dodkins

Book Designer Ania Bartoszek

Cover Researcher Naomi Parker

Thanks to Saralinda Turner

OUR STORY

A beat-up old car, a few dollars in the pocket and a sense of adventure. In 1972 that's all Tony and Maureen Wheeler needed for the trip of a lifetime – across Europe and Asia overland to Australia. It took several months, and at the end – broke but inspired – they sat at their kitchen table writing and stapling together their first travel guide, *Across Asia on the Cheap.* Within a week they'd sold 1500 copies. Lonely Planet was born.

Today, Lonely Planet has offices in Melbourne, London and Oakland, with more than 600 staff and writers. We share Tony's belief that 'a great guidebook should do three things: inform, educate and amuse'.

INDEX

000 Map pages
000 Photo pages

000 Map pages
000 Photo pages

OUR WRITERS

DAMIAN HARPER
With two degrees (one in modern and classical Chinese from SOAS), Damian has been writing for Lonely Planet for over two decades, contributing to titles as diverse as *China, Beijing, Shanghai, Vietnam, Thailand, Ireland, London, Mallorca, Malaysia, Singapore & Brunei, Hong Kong, France* and *Great Britain.* A seasoned guidebook writer, Damian has penned articles for numerous newspapers and magazines, including the *Guardian* and the *Daily Telegraph,* and currently makes Surrey, England, his home. A self-taught trumpet novice, his other hobbies include collecting modern first editions, photography and Taekwondo. Follow Damian on Instagram (damian.harper).

CATHERINE LE NEVEZ
Catherine's wanderlust kicked in when she roadtripped across Europe from her Parisian base, aged four, and she's been hitting the road at every opportunity since, travelling to around 60 countries and completing her Doctorate of Creative Arts in Writing, Masters in Professional Writing, and postgrad qualifications in Editing and Publishing along the way. Over the past dozen-plus years she's written scores of Lonely Planet guides and articles covering Paris, France, Europe and far beyond. Her work has also appeared in numerous online and print publications. Topping Catherine's list of travel tips is to travel without any expectations.

Published by Lonely Planet Publications Pty Ltd
ABN 36 005 607 983
2nd edition – June 2019
ISBN 978 1 78657 394 0
© Lonely Planet 2019   Photographs © as indicated 2019
10 9 8 7 6 5 4 3 2 1
Printed in China